Personnel and the Bottom Line

Personnel and the Bottom Line

Michael Armstrong

Institute of Personnel Management

For Clare, Ian and Emily Rose

First Published 1989

Photoset by HBM Typesetting Limited, Chorley, Lancs.
and printed in Great Britain by
Dotesios Printers Ltd, Trowbridge, Wiltshire.

British Library Cataloguing in Publication Data
Armstrong, Michael, *1928–*
   Personnel and the Bottom Line.
   1. Personnel Management
   I. Title II. Institute of Personnel Management
   658.3

   ISBN 0-85292-421-6

Contents

	Foreword	*vii*
	Acknowledgements	*ix*
	Introduction	*xi*
1	Management: the changing scene	1
2	The drive towards an entrepreneurial approach to personnel management	15
3	The entrepreneurial personnel function	30
4	Staffing the enterpreneurial personnel function	50
5	The entrepreneurial personnel director	55
6	The entrepreneurial personnel manager	70
7	The impact of the personnel function on the bottom line	79
8	Human resource strategy and the bottom line	91
9	Corporate culture and the bottom line	103
10	Organization planning and the bottom line	130
11	Competitive resourcing	136
12	Performance management and the bottom line	156
13	Quality and customer care	180
14	Gaining commitment	187
15	Personnel and the bottom line: conclusions	194
	Index	198

Foreword

When I was invited by the Institute of Personnel Management to write this book I readily agreed because it gave me a splendid opportunity to record my views on how personnel management should be integrated into the fabric of the business. As a General Manager and a member of the Executive Board of a highly successful enterprise for twelve years I have had the good fortune to play a full part in running the business as well as being responsible for the personnel function. What I learnt during this period was that personnel directors and managers are most effective when they are fully involved in the business at the strategic as well as the tactical level. And this book is mainly about how they can undertake this role effectively.

But I also realized that my experience at Book Club Associates, and previously as a management consultant, was interesting but limited. I therefore felt that I had to widen the scope of the book by obtaining the views of leading personnel professionals on how they and their departments were contributing to the bottom line. I was very fortunate in being able to enlist the help of twenty one personnel directors and other top personnel people who gladly spared the time to see me and give me their often frank and outspoken comments on the personnel scene as it is today and as it is developing. I believe that their contributions say more about what personnel management really is than anything I could write and I am most grateful to them for their help. Their names are listed overleaf.

I should also like to thank my wife, Peggy, for all her help in typing the manuscript and constructively criticizing my prose. Finally, I should like to express my gratitude to Anne Cordwent, my commissioning editor at the IPM for her invaluable guidance and support.

Acknowledgements

Grateful acknowledgement is given to the following for their important and lively contributions to this book:

Geoff Armstrong — Director, The MB Group plc (at the time of the interview, now Group Executive Director, Development Standard Chartered plc)

Don Beattie — Personnel Director, STC plc

Hank Bowen — Divisional Director, Staff and Training, W H Smith plc

Rhiannon Chapman — Director, Personnel, The International Stock Exchange

Nick Cowan — General Manager, Personnel TSB Bank plc, England and Wales Division

John Crosby — Director of Group Personnel, BAT Industries plc

Barry Curnow — Chairman and Chief Executive, MSL Group

Alan Fell — Director of Human Resources, The Heron Corporation plc

Peter Hobbs — Group Personnel Officer, The Wellcome Foundation Ltd.

John Hougham — Director of Personnel, Ford Motor Company

Terry Murphy — Managing Director, Miller/Ginsberg Murphy

Sir Leonard Peach — Chief Executive, NHS Management Board (at the time of the interview, now returned to IBM as Director of Personnel and Corporate Affairs)

Peter Reay	Group Personnel Director, Cadbury Schweppes plc (at the time of the interview, now retired)
Lynn Richards	Personnel Director, Halfords Ltd
Jeff Roberts	Personnel Director, Rumbelows Ltd
Gordon Sapsed	Senior Personnel Consultant, IBM United Kingdom Ltd
John Skae	Group Director (Resources), Legal and General Group plc
Mike Stanton	Director, Coopers & Lybrand Associates
Tony Vineall	Deputy Head of Personnel Division, Unilever plc
Peter Wickens	Director of Personnel and Information Systems Nissan Motor Manufacturing (UK) Ltd
Don Young	Group Personnel Director, Thorn EMI plc

Introduction

Personnel management is changing at an increasing rate. The rise of the human resource management movement is an indicator of this change, but there are many others. Words such as added value, competitive advantage, corporate culture, total quality and customer care, which were seldom mentioned ten years ago are now on everybody's lips. And this change is expressed in deeds as well as words. Personnel directors and managers are becoming involved in the business as never before. They are there when business strategies are evolved, playing their full part in ensuring that the human resource aspects are fully considered. They are there when plans are made for growth and increased profitability. And they are certainly there alongside their business colleagues in implementing these plans – ensuring that everything they do is directed to the improvement of bottom-line results.

This book is called 'Personnel and the Bottom Line' because profit is the ultimate measure of business performance. Of course personnel managers are very much concerned with investing in human assets which, even if they do not appear on the balance sheet, are in fact the company's most important capital. But assets are there to produce a return on what has been invested in them, and the prime responsibility of personnel people is to obtain the human assets the organization requires and then help to ensure that these *do* generate the profits needed to finance future growth, to keep the City and the shareholders happy and to fend off corporate predators.

Personnel management today is about improving performance, and it may be more appropriate to call personnel managers performance managers in future. Underlying this theme, however, is the belief that improved performance, as measured by the bottom line, benefits all those involved in the business: owners, managers, employees and, importantly, customers. The book does not claim that profit goals should be pursued by personnel managers or, indeed, any other managers at the expense of the interests of those concerned – the members of the organization and its customers. Business has social responsibilities to all its stakeholders, and personnel managers, even if they should not regard themselves as the consciences of the organization, have the duty to ensure, as far as they can, that these responsibilities are fulfilled.

This book starts with a general analysis of the changes taking place in the management scene and the impacts these changes are making on personnel management. These have resulted in the creation of a new breed of entrepreneurial personnel people, as is shown by the evidence of the twenty one interviews with top personnel professionals which form the core of the book.

The roles of the entrepreneurial personnel director and manager are then considered in broad terms and this leads into a general discussion of how personnel management can contribute to the bottom line. The rest of the book is devoted to more specific analyses of how this contribution can take effect in the fields of strategy, culture change, resourcing, performance management, quality and gaining commitment.

1 Management: The Changing Scene

This book is about change and the likely impact of change. The contribution that the personnel department can and should make to the bottom line has therefore to be assessed against the background of the changes that are taking place or are about to take place within the business environment and in organizations in the 1980s and 1990s.

The purpose of this chapter is, first, to review the environmental changes that have taken place or are likely to occur in the future. Secondly, an assessment will be made of the impact of these changes on attitudes, on organizations and management, and on the people who work in these organizations. Thirdly, consideration will be given to the problem of managing change. This will provide the framework for an analysis in the next chapter of what is happening to the personnel function within the changing context in which it operates.

ENVIRONMENTAL CHANGES

During the 1980s the economic and business environment became much more turbulent, uncertain and demanding. Tom Peters highlighted this in 1988 by calling his latest work *Thriving on chaos: handbook for a management revolution*.[1] In this book, he referred to 'an era of unprecedented uncertainty' and suggested that 'predictability is a thing of the past'.

Changes to the environment in which organizations operate are taking place rapidly in economic, political and social fields, in demographics, in the behaviour of customers, in the world of business generally, in technology and in management techniques.

Economic and political change

The most far-reaching change in recent years has been the rise of the enterprise culture and its associated phenomenon, the market economy.

1

There is, of course, nothing new in the concept. Adam Smith's most famous lines about capitalists, written in 1776 in *The wealth of nations*, were:

> In spite of their natural selfishness and rapacity, though they mean only their own conveniency, though the sole end which they proposed from the labours of all the thousands they employ, be the gratification of their own vain and insatiable desires . . . and without intending it, without knowing it, advance the interest of society.

And the advocate of self-help and self-reliance, Samuel Smiles wrote in 1859 that 'your own exertions are the key to life . . . Anything else – government policy, state intervention, group support – is incidental to the all-important effort made by each individual on his own behalf.' It is perhaps significant that *Self-help*, a paeon of praise to Victorian values, was republished in 1986 as a management classic, with an introduction by Sir Keith Joseph.[2]

More recently, George Gilder, the chief American philosopher of the enterprise culture, suggested that: 'Society is always in deep debt to the entrepreneurs who sustain it and rarely consume by themselves more than the smallest share of what they give society.'[3] He also wrote of his hero, the entrepreneur:

> He is not chiefly a tool of markets but a maker of markets; not a scout of opportunities but a developer of opportunity; not an optimizer of resources but an inventor of them; not a respondent to existing demands but an innovator who evokes demand.

The thrust of the Thatcher Government towards enterprise, innovation and self-sufficiency, its absolute belief in market forces, deregulation, the privatization programme, the 'big bang', the attack, largely successful, on trade union power, have all combined to create deep and lasting changes to the environment in which organizations operate and to corporate cultures and values.

Demographic change

It has been estimated that by 1999 the number of people in Great Britain between 16 and 19 years of age will fall by 25 per cent, that is 850,000. There will be a major shift in the age distribution of the working population and organizations will face real problems in recruiting young employees and trainees in the numbers that will be required.

Social change

Social changes take place within the context of economic and political developments. One of the most significant areas of change affecting organizations has been the rise of individualism and the relative decline of collectivism.

The trend towards individualism is partly a product of the enterprise culture which implies that nowadays it is everyone for him or herself. This does not mean that collectivism is dead. United we stand and divided we fall is still the underlining imperative for voluntarily joining trade unions or staff associations. But more and more people are expecting to be treated as individuals and not members of a crowd.

Another important area of social change has been the division of the nation into the 'haves' and 'have nots'. The 'haves' live in the more prosperous parts of the country and/or work in sectors of industry or commerce. The 'have nots' are unfortunate enough to live in the wrong place or work in the wrong industry. The 'haves' enjoy plenty of disposable income and want more. They are vociferous and demanding. The 'have nots' inevitably decline into apathy or anarchy. They no longer count, unless a foreign company, especially a Japanese one, seizes the opportunity to exploit under-used assets.

The change in consumer expectations

The market economy, prosperity (for some) and the increase in individual demands and needs have resulted in rising expectations from customers and consumers generally. They require not only cost-competitiveness but also higher standards of quality and service. They expect innovation in the development and provision of leading-edge products and services. And they demand the responsiveness of the small company, the corner shop, with the back-up that only large or efficient organizations can provide. If they don't get what they want, they have plenty of choice elsewhere and they will exercise the right to make that choice.

Changes in the business environment

The business environment has changed widely and significantly over the last decade in the following areas:

- *Growth:* this is now the driving force, often as a result of stock market pressures which sometimes encourage directors to safeguard short-term performance, as measured by earnings per share, at the expense of longer-term developments.

- *Takeovers and acquisitions:* these present an increasing threat to existing managements but can concentrate their minds wonderfully on introducing changes designed to increase the profitability of their businesses. Again, this is sometimes achieved by prejudicing the scope for future prosperity. If the defence fails and the merger or acquisition takes place, then imposed changes in management and the business itself are almost inevitable.

- *Increased competition:* the decline in certain sectors of the manufacturing industry in Great Britain such as consumer electronics products, vehicles and machine tools is well known. Competition is fierce, at home and abroad. It is now global, and multi-national corporations have the ability to switch production between countries and even continents. 1992 presents an opportunity but also a threat. The vogue phrases of the 1980s were 'competitive edge' and 'niche marketing'.

The former is achieved by innovation, flexibility, efficiency and being responsive to customer needs. As Theodore Levitt wrote:

> The organization must learn to think of itself not as producing goods or services but as *buying customers*, as doing the thing that will make people *want* to do business with it.[4]

Niche marketing involves identifying segments of the market or groups of customers that fit the skills and resources available to the company. These segments and customers are then targeted with differentiated products or services which offer variety in the marketplace and have features which distinguish them from their competitors. The marketing process defines the needs of potential customers and then exerts influence on their wants so that they are translated into demands. The tendency is to move from mass marketing into niche marketing, which has considerable influence on the ways in which firms develop, manufacture and sell their products or services.

- *The Japanese phenomenon:* explanations of the Japanese miracle abound. Some say it is due to the consistent, conservative, macroeconomic climate in which companies, their bankers and the Government work together well as a team. Others, like Pascale and Athos,[5] argue that the major reason for the superiority of the Japanese is simply their managerial skill, which includes the extraordinary and consistent way in which all the components of Japanese organizations fit together. Others emphasize lifetime employment and shared values as the key factors. Yet others, such as Korean writer O-Young Lee, suggest that the Japanese tradition of smallness and sensitivity to information 'perfectly positions them to take the lead in the coming age of reductionism'.[6] Nissan, in its publication *Things you want to know about Nissan and Japan*, as quoted by Peter Wickens in *The road to Nissan*,[7] states that: 'The Japanese people tend to value group harmony more than individuality.' Wickens writes about the Nissan tripod developed for their plant in Washington, Tyne and Wear, the three legs of which are flexibility, quality consciousness and team working. These, together with the emphasis on using time effectively, are probably the most important contributions that the Japanese approach is making to changing management styles in Great Britain.

- *Innovation:* product life cycles are shorter and leading-edge firms must innovate to remain competitive and to establish and maintain a prominent place in their market niches. This means harnessing technological and other resources to exploit opportunities and to capitalize on strengths.

- *Flexibility:* a turbulent economic environment, volatile exchange rates, the pressure for growth, increased competition, the need to respond quickly to marketing opportunities, the emphasis on innovation – these all combine to enforce flexibility, to recognize that stability is a thing of the past and to create an environment in which the ability to respond quickly to, and to manage change, is a requisite for success.

New technology

The most obvious and most significant developments in new technology from the point of view of the management of organizations and their human resources are, of course, taking place in the field of information technology. This is becoming an integral part of the management process, in so far as that process is largely concerned with information flows.

Computer-based technologies in other activities, such as computer-aided design, computer-aided manufacture, database marketing, point-of-sale retail outlet systems linked to central inventory, accounts and distribution, human resource planning and computer-based training are also changing radically the ways in which organizations, and the people who work in them, function.

Artificial intelligence (AI) will be commonly used in the more sophisticated firms of the future. This can be defined as the attempt to make machines achieve human capabilities such as seeing, hearing and thinking. For business purposes, the most relevant application of AI is the expert system. This is a computer program that mimics the behaviour of an expert. Expert systems can solve difficult problems, explain the result, learn, restructure knowledge and determine relevance. And they know what they don't know. They can be used to solve tough problems like contract estimation or air freight scheduling. The American Express Company, for example, uses an expert system to help its credit authorization staff sort through as many as 13 data bases. Coopers & Lybrand has an expert system that helps accountants to review the way their clients accrue taxes and to offer tax planning advice. One report has suggested that in the 1990s, nine out of 10 British firms will be using expert systems.[8]

Management techniques

New management techniques are springing up all the time. Some become flavour of the month and are later discredited, for good or bad reasons. Management by objectives and OD (organizational development) are cases in point. More recently, techniques and management methods such as just-in-time (JIT) or time-based competition (TBC) have achieved prominence.

Just-in-time, a system originating in the Japanese automobile industry, sequences operations through a number of small units. Each unit delivers to the next unit precisely what that unit requires to carry out the next stage of manufacture and just in time for that work to start, thus reducing work-in-progress to an absolute minimum and preventing delays and bottlenecks.

Time-based competition recognizes the precept that companies have to move fast to win business these days. Research undertaken by the Boston Consulting Group has shown that many of the world's most successful companies are taking advantage of a new source of competitive advantage, a recognition by their managements of the value of time. Companies such as Toyota who apply this recognition to every element of their business, from initial order to final delivery, are known as 'time-based competitors'. They are characterized by their ability to use systematic analytical techniques and supporting computer technology to differentiate key or main sequence tasks from support functions, and then reduce the time it takes to perform them throughout the organization. Computer and telecommunications technologies are making it possible to shorten substantially the time taken between order and delivery. Time-based competitors make main sequence activities self-regulatory and so reduce supervisory functions. They employ a much smaller number of people in support functions than companies that have not adopted this approach, and the customer-driven proportion of the organization is bigger.

THE IMPACT OF CHANGE

The impact of change needs to be considered under three headings:

1 *Attitudes:* how views about the ways in which organizations should be managed are being reconsidered.

2 *Organization and management:* the new forms of organization and the different approaches to management that are evolving as a result of environmental and technological change.

3 *People:* the new demands made on people at work, the new ways in which people are working in or for organizations and the new approaches required for the management of people.

Attitudes

The 1980s saw the coming of what might be described as the new managerial revolution. It emerged from the environmental changes described above, but its essence was captured by a number of best-selling writers such as Athos, Geneen, Gilder, Iococca, Harvey-Jones, Kanter, Ouchi, Pascale, Peters, Walton and Waterman. Their views and sayings have become part of the standard vocabulary of management, often by some process of osmosis, and have resulted in attitudinal shifts in the following areas.

● *The marketplace:* it is at last fully recognized that organizations are market-driven and that management must be market-orientated.

- *Customers:* the word customer is on everyone's lips. Customer care and service programmes have become a major feature in the personnel strategies of firms as diverse as British Airways, W H Smith and Rumbelows.

- *Profitability:* increasingly, profitability is accepted as the main goal at all levels in organizations, and not just at the top. This belief has arisen partly as a result of the general climate produced by the enterprise culture and partly by the intensive efforts made by many managements to communicate the importance of profits to their employees. Those who ignore this message and fail to be profit-conscious at all times do so at their peril. And this applies as much to personnel people as anyone else.

- *Excellence:* the publication in 1982 of *In search of excellence* by Tom Peters and Robert Waterman[9] initiated what became almost a cult of excellence. In *A passion for excellence*[10] Tom Peters suggested that the two sustaining edges of excellence were superior customer service and constant innovation. But these had to be built on 'a bedrock of listening, trust and respect for the dignity and the creative potential of each person in the organization'. And the overriding element that connects all the others, according to Peters, is leadership, 'which means vision, cheerleading, enthusiasm, love, trust, verve, passion, obsession, consistency . . . out and out drama, (and the management thereof), creating heroes at all levels, coaching, effectively walking around and numerous other things.'

ICL, in its message to all its employees, *The ICL way: the way we do things around here*, defined its commitment to excellence as follows:

> ICL's sights are now set on world success. That demands excellence in everything we undertake. And excellence will be achieved only by adopting 'can do' attitudes and the highest levels of co-operation and teamwork right through the company . . .
>
> Every new task demands that we set and agree standards of excellence, define the ways in which those standards are to be met, and then go to achieve them without compromise.
>
> Only by doing that, day in, day out, can we expect to make real progress as individuals or as a company in the highly competitive world markets of the future.

- *Turbulence:* possibly as a result of the poor subsequent performance of some of the 'excellent' companies he analyzed with Robert Waterman in 1982, Tom Peters refined his definition of excellence in 1988 to read:

> Excellent firms don't believe in excellence – only in constant improvement and constant change. That is, excellent firms of tomorrow will cherish impermanence and thrive on chaos.[1]

Managements are beginning to accept turbulence as a way of life. They aim, indeed, to capitalize on it by, in Peter Drucker's immortal phrase, recognizing that 'there are no problems, only opportunities'. They try to avoid crises but if, inevitably, they do arise, they use crisis management techniques not only to get themselves out of trouble but also, and while the adrenalin flows, as a springboard for future growth.

Lee Iacocca, when dealing with the Chrysler crisis in 1978, started off with the motto 'If you stand still in this business, you get run over very quickly.' Interestingly, however, his solution to the problems of Chrysler's massive losses was people-centred:

> These problems were urgent, and their solutions all pointed in the same direction. I needed a good team of experienced people who could work with me in turning this company around before it finally fell apart. My highest priority was to put the team together before it was too late.[11]

The firm of the 90s

Environmental and technological developments have resulted in fundamental changes to the ways in which firms are structured and managed. We now have:

- *The responsive firm* – which has to react quickly to changes in the marketplace and in customer needs and preferences.

- *The pro-active firm* – which has to make markets as well as adapt itself to them.

- *The flexible firm* – which has to be able to adjust its structure, its product range, its marketing strategies, its manufacturing and distribution systems and facilities quickly either to respond to, or to anticipate, change.

- *The information-based firm* – which will be knowledge-orientated and composed largely of specialists who direct and discipline their own performance through organized feedback from colleagues, customers and the strategic business units into which the organization is divided in accordance with the markets they serve. Peter Drucker wrote in 1988 that 'information is data endowed with relevance and purpose'.[12] He suggested that to ensure that the right sort of information is available, and thus clarify the direction in which the organization should go, organizations will require more specialists in operations, where the work will be done by task-focused teams, and fewer in the centre.

- *The compact firm* – in which layers of superfluous management and supervision, have been removed, forcing top management to concentrate on strategic planning and overall control and giving more scope for action at operational levels. This development has partly arisen from a natural revulsion to top-heavy and over-managed organizations. The extended use of information technology has had an important effect. As Drucker pointed out:

> Whole layers of management neither make decisions nor lead. Instead their main, if not their only, function is to serve as 'relays' – human boosters for the faint, unfocused signals that pass for communications in the traditional pre-information organization.[12]

- *The decentralized firm* – which consists of strategic business units placed firmly in their market niches and capable of responding quickly to opportunities and threats. The units are compact and tightly managed to achieve well-defined goals with the minimum of direction from above.

- *The leaner firm* – which has been created by the processes of concentrating work at local levels, eliminating unnecessary layers of management, decimating headquarters staff and replacing generalists with specialists.

- *The cohesive firm* – differentiation, decentralization, even fragmentation, does not necessarily result in disintegration. The elimination of management layers, the opening up of communications and the requirement to re-group to meet new demands combine to break down barriers and to impose the need for a more cohesive approach. Flat organizations require more involvement horizontally between task-focused teams. Top management has to make greater efforts than ever before to achieve integration and a sense of common purpose through mission statements, the development and dissemination of core values, and cultural change programmes. Harold Geneen, Chief Executive of the International Telephone and Telegraph Company (ITT), stressed the need to cut through the formal structure so that the managers of the autonomous subsidiaries would think of ITT as 'one company, one team, one group of managers heading in the same direction'.[13]

- *The performance-based firm* – more than ever before the emphasis is on performance, on accountability for results and on the achievement of well-defined and demanding goals. Harold Geneen summed up his own business philosophy in his three-sentence course on business management: 'You read a book from beginning to end. You run a business in the opposite way. You start with the end, and then you do everything you must to reach it.' This bias towards action and performance is the driving force for the achievement of better bottom-line results, that is, increased profitability. It is a force that personnel people cannot afford to ignore.

- *The global firm* – the extension of business worldwide means that companies have to adopt a global approach to managing their affairs. The history of Motorola is of steady progression from USA domestic activities (1928–48), to an international presence (1948–80), to global operation (1980 into the future). The global approach, as explained by Motorola's Patrick Canavan, is 'a mindset supported by operating principles'. It is far more than just trading across national boundaries. It involves planning integrated marketing and manufacturing operations in any part of the world where opportunities exist, and developing managers who can switch rapidly between continents and, incidentally, between functions. Global management is also flexible and responsive management.

People

The impact of environmental changes on the people who work in organizations takes the following forms:

1 *The movement from control to commitment*. As Richard Walton pointed out in his *Harvard Business Review* article 'From control to commitment in the workplace[14],' the traditional model for management is 'To establish order, and achieve efficiency in the application of the workforce.' This is replaced by the commitment strategy in which 'performance expectations are high and serve not to define minimum standards but to provide "stretch objectives", emphasize continuous improvement and reflect the requirements of the marketplace.' In this new commitment-based approach to managing people:

> Jobs are designed to be broader than before, to combine planning and implementation, and to include efforts to upgrade operations, not just maintain them. Individual responsibilities are expected to change as conditions change, and teams, not individuals, often are the organizational units accountable for performance. With management hierarchies relatively flat and differences in status minimized, control and lateral co-ordination depend on shared goals, and expertise, rather than formal position, determines influence.

Walton therefore recognizes that, although individuality is important to cope with uncertainty, manage change and react quickly, the new flat, lean and flexible organizations rely more heavily on teamwork than ever before. The apparent paradox of pressures for individualism as well as for teamwork is one of the many areas of ambiguity that personnel people have to live with.

2 *Individualism*. The organization needs teamwork and people will enjoy working in cohesive groups, but they still like to be treated as individuals. John Harvey-Jones made this point when he wrote:

> In the organization that switches its people on, the individual is king. He feels that he is trusted, respected as an individual, treated as one and rewarded as one, and that it is his individuality that is needed: his individual contribution, rather than conformity to some sort of ideal 'company' man.[15]

3 *Paying for performance*. The enterprise culture demands that people should be paid as individuals in accordance with their contribution. Paying

for performance is seen not only as a reward but also as a key motivating device. As Rosabeth Moss Kanter said in the *Harvard Business Review* in 1987:

> More and more senior executives are trying to turn their employees into entrepreneurs – people who earn a direct return on the value they create. . . . By creating new forms for identifying, recognizing and ultimately permitting contributions, the attack on pay goes beyond pay to colour relationships. In the process, the iron cage of bureaucracy is being rattled in ways that will eventually change the nature and the meaning of the hierarchy in ways we cannot yet imagine.[16]

4　*The threat to equity*. Performance-related pay erodes historic incremental payment systems, as in the Civil Service and many private sector bureaucracies. These systems have always been defended by white collar trade unions because they are perceived to be equitable, that is, all staff are dealt with equally. But equity is about being fair, not about treating everyone exactly alike, so that they get the same increment, however well they perform. Those who favour performance-related pay do so because they think it is fairer to pay good performers better than poor performers. People should not be rewarded, they say, simply for being there.

The market economy has also damaged the principle of equity. In all sectors of the economy it has had to be recognized that people in some occupations have a scarcity value. To attract and retain them it is therefore necessary to pay them more than their colleagues in jobs which are of a similar value to the organization if internal relativities were the only consideration.

5　*The nature of work*. New technology, changes in the social climate and new types of organizational structure have together caused major changes to the composition of the workforce. The move towards multi-skilling to enhance flexibility will accelerate. In the field of job design, autonomy, based on the use of information technology will increase, whether it is individuals working in what Alvin Toffler calls their 'electronic cottages' or autonomous working groups.

High-performance work design will become the most frequently used job design technique. This approach will define competencies and stress the performance requirements of jobs in terms of objectives, targets and standards of performance. Jobs will be designed around individuals or within the context of autonomous working groups with these performance requirements uppermost in people's minds.

Other key developments in the nature of work as listed by Charles Handy include:[17]

• many more people than at present not working in an organization through an increase in the number of out-workers and in sub-contracting facilitated by information technology in the shape of computer networks;

- fewer mammoth bureaucracies, more federal organizations, and more small businesses;
- more importance given to the informal, uncounted economy of the home and the community;
- a smaller working population and a larger dependent population.

A further development has been the increased proportion of technical, professional and commercial staff employed in organizations. In Siemens AG, for example, the proportion of such staff in 1962 was 33 per cent of the workforce. By 1986 this proportion had become 53 per cent.

6 *Competences*. The pressure for competency (a word 'discovered' in management circles in the 1980s) has resulted in new approaches to defining training needs and designing relevant training programmes. It has also led to an emphasis on 'performance management', which requires managers not only to assess the performance of their staff but also to do something about it.

7 *Careers*. Individuals still want career opportunities, possibly more so than ever before. But flatter organizations and the increase in the proportion of specialists and scientific and professional staff means that career paths are obscure or end too quickly.

PROBLEMS

The changes discussed above create a number of problems for personnel managers. The following questions need to be answered:

(a) How do we create unified vision in an organization of specialists?

(b) How can we devise and maintain the management structure for an organization of task forces?

(c) How can we obtain commitment to achieving the objectives of the organization, including quality and high levels of customer service, when we are more and more appealing to individual motivating factors, including personal greed?

(d) How are we going to get and to keep the high-level performers we need, especially when facing the demographic problems of the 1990s?

(e) How are we going to provide career structures for specialists, scientists and professional staff in the flatter organizations?

(f) How can we reconcile the conflicting demands of internal equity and external competitiveness when fixing salaries?

(g) How do we manage the organization of the future with its increasing proportion of part-timers, contract workers and home-workers or 'tele-commuters'?

(h) How are we going to get the performance improvements needed to obtain the 'bottom-line' results the organization is expected to achieve?

(i) How are we going to get people to work in the global organization and to accept that an international approach to management is required?

(j) How will we be able to get employees to accept that operational flexibility has to be a way of life for them in organizations which must not only exist but must also thrive in a turbulent and sometimes chaotic market economy?

These questions can only be satisfactorily answered if radical approaches to the practice of personnel management are adopted. The premise from which all necessary developments in personnel management must be inferred is that the role of personnel directors or personnel managers should be to do everything they can to improve organizational performance and thus achieve better bottom-line results.

This means, first, understanding what is required to create and maintain an effective organization as measured by the results it achieves. Secondly, it involves ensuring that people are treated as the organization's key resource and taking whatever steps are required as partners in the business to see that it gets, keeps and develops the committed human resources it needs.

The drive towards an entrepreneurial approach to personnel management is discussed in the next chapter against the background of these changes to the management scene.

References

1 PETERS, Tom. *Thriving on chaos: handbook for a management revolution*. London, Macmillan, 1988

2 SMILES, Samuel. *Self-help*. London, Sidgwick & Jackson, 1986 (first published 1859)

3 GILDER, George. *The spirit of enterprise*. London, Viking, 1985

4 LEVITT, Theodore. *The marketing imagination*. New York, The Free Press, 1983

5 PASCALE, Richard *and* ATHOS, Anthony. *The art of Japanese management*. London, Sidgwick & Jackson, 1986

6 O-YOUNG, Lee. *Smaller is better: Japan's mastery of the miniature*. New York, Kodansha International, 1984

7 WICKENS, Peter. *The road to Nissan*. London, Macmillan, 1987

8 'Boom in expert systems forecast'. *Management News*. May 1987. p5

9 PETERS, Tom *and* WATERMAN, Robert. *In search of excellence*. New York, Harper & Row, 1982

10 PETERS, Tom *and* AUSTIN, Nancy. *A passion for excellence*. London, Collins, 1985
11 IACOCCA, Lee. *Iacocca: an autobiography*. London, Sidgwick & Jackson, 1985
12 DRUCKER, Peter. 'The coming of the new organization'. *Harvard Business Review*. January–February 1988, pp 45–53
13 GENEEN, Harold. *Managing*. London, Granada, 1985
14 WALTON, Richard. 'From control to commitment in the workplace'. *Harvard Business Review*. March–April 1985, pp 77–84
15 HARVEY-JONES, John. *Making it happen*. Glasgow, Collins, 1988
16 KANTER, Rosabeth Moss. 'The attack on pay'. *Harvard Business Review*. March–April 1987
17 HANDY, Charles. *The future of work*. Oxford, Blackwell, 1984

2 The Drive Towards an Entrepreneurial Approach to Personnel Management

The French economist J B Say coined the word 'entrepreneur' around 1800 when he wrote that: 'The entrepreneur shifts economic resources out of the area of lower and into an area of higher productivity and greater yield.' Closer to our own time, George Gilder in *The spirit of enterprise* said that entrepreneurs 'create wealth and employment. They take exception to the received view that companies should be market led. *They* lead the market.'[1]

Entrepreneurs:

- Conceive business visions and turn them into profitable realities.

- Base their achievements on the strength of their vision.

- 'Inhabit a world where the last becomes first, where supply creates demand, where belief precedes knowledge.' (George Gilder)

- Are action orientated; in the words of Peters and Waterman, 'They do it, fix it, try it'.[2]

- Have the gift of visualizing the steps from idea to actualization.

- Are both thinkers and doers, planners and workers.

- Can tolerate ambiguity; 'Enterprise always consists of action in uncertainty.' (George Gilder)

- See themselves as responsible for their own destiny; they are dedicated, setting self-determined goals.

- Believe in creating markets for their ideas, not just in responding to existing market demands.

- Understand absolutely that all their efforts are directed towards innovation, achieving a competitive edge and profitable growth as measured by the bottom line.

The entrepreneurial personnel manager is very much concerned with added value, ensuring by leadership and positive advice that the maximum return is obtained by the organization from its investment in human resources, shifting them, as Say said, from an area of lower to an area of higher yield.

This chapter explores the growth of the concept of entrepreneurial personnel management by means of:

1 An analysis of the impact on personnel management of the changes discussed in Chapter 1.

2 A review of the changing scene as perceived by leading personnel directors and commentators on personnel management.

3 An examination of the various models of personnel management which have evolved recently in response to the changing scene.

4 A specific study of the human resource model which became prominent in the 1980s and is still much discussed although, as Nick Cowan said in January 1988:[3]

> We should not continue to waste time and effort in debating whether we are engaged in human resource management or in personnel management. Personally, I think Michael Armstrong effectively ended the debate when he wrote:[4] 'HRM is perceived as a total approach to the strategic management of a key resource which has to be the responsibility of the board, with advice from personnel specialists. Personnel management provides that advice and the services required to implement the plans.'

5 An analysis of the new entrepreneurial model, with its emphasis on performance and added value, which complements rather than replaces the human resource model.

THE IMPACT OF CHANGE ON PERSONNEL MANAGEMENT

The key areas of change affecting personnel manangement are:

- *The enterprise culture*, with its philosophy of 'go for growth', its individualism, its orientation to the marketplace and, above all, its belief that the ultimate success of the company is measured by its bottom-line performance. If personnel managers want to help their firms achieve a competitive edge and make a real contribution to organizational success, then they have to operate within this culture. The work of the personnel function, in Terry Murphy's words, 'has to become part of the business fabric'.

- *The organizational context*, where structures are flatter, leaner and decentralized. The old top-heavy organization with a massive personnel department is becoming a thing of the past. Companies are now structuring their organizations much more closely around their markets. Personnel managers have to respond more quickly to market forces.

- *The flexible and responsive firm*, that is emerging as a result of competitive pressures, means that personnel managers must be faster on their feet and more capable of adjusting their role to meet rapidly changing demands in conditions of turbulence. Personnel bureaucracies are vanishing.

- *Quality* – the pursuit of quality and excellence in every aspect of the company's operations, but especially with regard to customer care, has placed a heavy onus on the personnel function to help in the development of corporate cultures where these core values are accepted by everyone as 'the way we do things around here'.

- *The changing pattern of work*, with its emphasis on flexibility, multi-skilling and team building, and the increased use of contract workers and part-timers, is forcing organizations and their personnel managers to re-think the ways in which people are recruited, trained, developed, motivated and deployed.

- *Global firms*, which are becoming more and more prominent, require their personnel people to think and act internationally. A parochial, self-contained approach is no longer appropriate.

- *New technology*, with its impact on methods of working and organization sturctures, raises special problems for personnel managers who have to cope with change and the nervous reactions of employees to it.

- *Commitment* by all concerned to the organization's objectives and values has been recognized as a key ingredient for success. Richard Walton has coined the phrase 'from control to commitment'.[5] Personnel managers are now expected to contribute to the formulation and implementation of strategies designed to enhance the identification of employees with the organization. 'Mutuality' in relationships between managements and their employees has become all-important.

Implications for personnel management

To make an effective contribution to the bottom line – the ultimate success criterion – personnel managers have to become business partners. They are becoming performance managers rather than personnel managers, bearing in mind, of course, that performance is achieved through people. They are also having to become, in Rosabeth Moss Kanter's phrase,[6] 'change masters, helping and guiding the organization, its management and all who work in it to manage and, indeed, to exploit and triumph over change.'

Barry Curnow referred to these changes and the role of the personnel function when he said:

I see all sorts of economic, market and environmental changes taking place in which the personnel function, or perhaps I should say the best personnel viewpoint, is often not located in the personnel department. It's often most clearly seen in a personnel-minded chief executive or managing director who sometimes has spent a spell in the personnel department. But what I see that really distinguishes the best from the rest is where you have a very people-minded business leader who understands that you compete through getting and keeping the best people and through creating a company climate and atmosphere and ethos in which it is exciting and attractive for people to work.

If, and quite rightly, it is the business leader who, through his or her vision, determines the organization's mission, masterminds its strategies and creates its values, where does this leave the personnel function? The rest of this chapter addresses this question.

PERSONNEL MANAGEMENT: THE CHANGING SCENE

Changes to the personnel management scene are taking place in the following areas:

- an emphasis on people as a key resource
- a recognition that the personnel function must be totally involved in the business as a generator of added value
- the emergence of the principle of mutuality
- a reduction in the prominence of industrial relations as a priority in the work of personnel departments
- a growth in the personnel profession and more recognition, in some quarters, of the positive role that personnel people can play.

People as a key resource

Increasingly, employees are being regarded as assets rather than as costs. They are seen as one of the key resources of an organization, if not *the* key resource, about which investment decisions have to be made and upon which the future success of the enterprise depends.

Rhiannon Chapman made the point that:

> The personnel issue is essentially a balance sheet issue rather than a P & L issue because you are dealing with investments – asset management.

Asset management in this sense is undoubtedly a vital role for personnel managers. But the profit and loss account is still important. A satisfactory bottom-line return on these assets has to be obtained if the business is to grow or even survive in its present form. There are lots of financial predators about who will pounce on a firm whose return on assets employed and earnings per share leave something to be desired. And City commentators will be scathing about any company whose bottom-line performance does not meet their high expectations. This can lead to difficulty in obtaining finance to provide for future growth or the threat of a takeover, with all the ensuing trouble, expense and anxiety.

Involvement of the personnel function in the business

If the importance of people as a key resource is recognized then, as John Hougham said:

> The role [of the personnel function] is completely indistinguishable from the mainstream business. In no sense is it a staff add-on.

From the organization's point of view, therefore, its employees, like any other resource, are a means to an end. The management of them is not an end in itself.

As Peter Wickens commented:

> We are not in the human relations business, we are not in the cost control business, we are not in the industrial engineering business. We are in the business of building cars of the right quality to the right schedule that the customer will want to buy at a price that will enable us to generate the income we need to invest for future growth. That's the business we're in.

People are employed to ensure that organizations achieve their objectives in a market economy and in the face of severe competition. In this connection, a paper on perspectives and objectives presented at a Cadbury Schweppes international personnel conference stated that:

> The Cadbury Schweppes personnel function exists to provide individual companies and the group as a whole with a competitive advantage. The job is to help colleagues find, motivate and grow the sort of people who will achieve Cadbury Schweppes short- and long-term aims, and to do so cost-effectively. As in every other function, the test is that it contributes to the performance of the business, its relevance and the value for money it offers.

This definition was prefaced with the words 'to state the obvious'. But it is not all that obvious in many firms, even today. Personnel departments and their managers lose credibility if they do not respond appropriately to the need to operate at the leading edge and to maintain competitive success. But changes are taking place, as was established by a Warwick University research team which concluded in 1988 that the firms they studied had introduced significant developments in their human resource management practices under competitive pressure: 'A complex set of business environment changes have led to a series of generic, strategic responses.'[7] These were particularly evident in the fields of 'competitive restructuring, decentralization, internationalization, acquisition and merger, technological change and new concepts of service provision and distribution.'

Shifts in assumptions about how people should be managed

There have been a number of shifts in the assumptions which govern how people should be managed and how relationships with employees should be developed and maintained. As defined by Michael Beer and Bert Spector these are:[8]

1   Organizations are viewed as systems, whose effectiveness in terms of transforming inputs to outputs is achieved by developing a fit between the various components in the system (functions and people) and between the system and its environment.

2   There is a long-term coincidence of interest between all the stakeholders in an organization.

3   Power equalization is a key to encouraging openness and collaboration amongst stakeholders.

4   People are capable of growth in terms of skills, values and commitment if and when the work environment encourages it.

5   Employees will be motivated and the organization more effective if the workforce considers the objectives to be legitimate.

6   Open communication builds trust and commitment.

7   People who participate in defining problems and solutions will become committed to the new directions that result from the process of participation.

Mutuality

What is emerging from these shifts is an overriding principle, that of mutuality, which may be defined as a common interest in corporate excellence. This means unleashing the latent creativity and energies of people throughout the business by emphasizing common interests, gaining understanding and acceptance of the mission and core values of the organization and increasing commitment by involving people in its affairs. It requires the creation of mutual influence mechanisms which facilitate change, encourage flexibility and lead to improvements in performance and better bottom-line results. Tom Peters summarized this view as follows:

> Trust people and treat them like adults, enthuse them by lively and imaginative leadership, develop and demonstrate an obsession for quality, make them feel they own the business, and your workforce will respond with total commitment. [9]

Decreased emphasis on industrial relations

Policies of mutuality aim to elicit employee commitment and thus improve organizational effectiveness. They have been influenced by the preference for an individualistic (enterprise) ideology rather than a collectivist one. The result has been a shift away from industrial relations concerned only with trade union members, first to employee relations covering all staff, and then onwards to the development of commitment strategies where the emphasis is on mutuality.

In response to a question about where the personnel function is going, Tony Vineall said that:

> The obvious thing to start with is the enormous change in the preoccupation of personnel people. I've been a personnel manager for 30 years and for much of that time our lives were dominated by indusrial relations, pay policies, rates of pay for manual workers and so on. By and large that has changed. It hasn't disappeared but it's no longer of overriding importance. I think, to be honest, that some personnel managers are a bit lost without it. Their role in their company really operated on a fulcrum of industrial relations conflict. I remember a personnel director of an engineering company saying to me quite plaintively that it was three months since his board had discussed a strike. Personnel directors, in fact all personnel people, are talking much more about the things that they always said should be their strategic contribution to the business. They are talking about the development of human resources, especially the fast-track people who are going places. They are talking about the reward package for these people and beyond that, the total culture, climate and style of the business. This move from trench warfare about pay with trade unions to a preoccupation with the supply of talent and the motivation of that talent in the organization is a major change.

Personnel management: growth and recognition

The recognition of human resources as assets not costs, the move towards policies of mutuality and the consequential opening up of the arena of personnel management referred to by Tony Vineall have together created increased opportunities for growth and recognition in the personnel profession. John Crosby commented that:

> The first thing that one notices if one has been in personnel for some time is the actual physical growth of the personnel management function. . . . Where has this growth come from? I think part of it is organic, the progressive realization that personnel is a key part of the business. The other part, though, is the physical spreading of personnel management as a cohesive activity into where it simply didn't belong or exist before. I suppose the classic example would be the public sector where personnel as a regularized profession has spread into local government and the health service and is recognized by the Civil Service as a distinct area of activity.

On the subject of recognition, Peter Reay remarked that:

> The most satisfying thing in my work in this company (Cadbury Schweppes) in recent years has been the way in which the personnel function has been recognized and has been, as it were, empowered and given greater authority and support by the line.

He went on to illustrate this by saying that another rewarding aspect for him in his business was the fact that:

> We hold a biennial international personnel directors' conference, for all our personnel directors worldwide, and there are actually about 20 people who now have that title, all of whom are on the boards of their company. And that's quite different from 10 to 15 years ago when the personnel manager was typically reporting to a production manager or something.

The personnel directors interviewed by the writer when preparing this book were generally in agreement about the increasing significance of the new-look personnel management (or human resource management if you prefer the term) in British industry. But this view is not held generally. David Guest has suggested that 'if HRM (human resource management) is to be taken seriously, personnel managers must give it away.'[10] And he went on to comment that 'in the USA the prevailing view appears to be that HRM is too important to be left to personnel managers.'

In 1986 Shaun Tyson and Alan Fell suggested that there was a crisis in personnel management arising from, amongst other things:[11]

- a failure to understand the function which has led to the appointment of amateurs, or failures, to a task which requires considerable analytical and personal skills

- a lack of agreement on what human resource management is or what it should be

- the fact that personnel management in the UK has failed to generate, or be asociated with, an overall set of social, political and economic objectives which are acceptable to the major economic decision-makers.

The last point is particularly important. Geoff Armstrong has remarked that in his opinion the principle that personnel management could and should make a major contribution to the bottom line was generally accepted. But other people in less sophisticated organizations have different views, summed up by one general manager who thought that a book entitled 'Personnel and the bottom line' would be a very slim volume indeed!

This is a key issue and the first step in dealing with it is to look at the various models of personnel management that have been developed recently.

PERSONNEL MANAGEMENT MODELS

Shaun Tyson and Alan Fell suggest[11] that there are three basic personnel management models:

1 The 'clerk of works' model. In this model all authority for action is vested in line managers. 'Personnel policies are formed or created after the actions which created the need.' Policies are not integral to the business and are short term and *ad hoc*. Authority is vested in line managers and personnel activities are largely routine – employment and day-to-day administration.

2 The 'contracts manager' model. In this model policies are well established, often implicit, with a heavy industrial relations emphasis, possibly derived from an employer's association. The personnel department will use fairly sophisticated systems, especially in the field of employee relations. The personnel manager is likely to be a professional or very experienced in industrial relations. He (or, more unlikely, she) will not be on the board and, although having some authority to 'police' the implementation of policies, acts mainly in an interpretive, not a creative or innovative, role.

3 The 'architect' model. In this model explicit personnel policies exist as part of the corporate strategy. Human resource planning and development are important concepts and a long-term view is taken. Systems tend to be sophisticated. The head of the personnel function is probably on the board and his or her power is derived from professionalism and perceived contribution to the business.

Of course, like all models, these can only provide a generalized view of the different roles of personnel managers. They overlap in many organizations and exist in different ways in different parts of large or diversified companies. But there is a continuum between those situations where personnel management is a routine, administrative, relatively lowly and reactive function to those where it is sophisticated, high-powered and pro-active. Where a personnel function is placed on the continuum depends partly on the extent to which those at the top really believe in a 'human resource management' approach which recognizes that people are *the* resource and have to be dealt with strategically. It also depends on the professionalism, sheer ability and determination to exercise influence of whoever heads the personnel function.

It is possible to provide some historical perspective on the development of the personnel function by reference to the model shown in Figure 2.1. This traces three streams of development leading to human resource management:

1 *The personnel management stream*, which springs from the beginnings of personnel management in the welfare department and goes on through personnel administration to the broader field of personnel management, with its extended deployment of techniques such as management by objectives, job evaluation, psychometric testing and merit rating.

2 *The human relations/behavioural science stream*, which starts with the human relations school, as influenced by people such as Elton Mayo and Kurt Lewin, and develops into the behavioural science movement. This was the Argyris, Herzberg, Likert and McGregor era when the major concerns were with the quality of working like, organizational health and effectiveness and OD (organization development) 'interventions'. The behavioural science movement also influenced developments in the more traditional personnel administration and employee relations areas.

3 *The industrial relations stream*, which starts with the traditional IR department, moves into employee relations, complete with productivity deals and structured communication programmes, and goes on to the field of mutuality where, with some influence from Japan, the emphasis is on developing a sense of common purpose.

These three streams converge into the human resource management pool. This is also fed by the excellence factor and the Japanese connection. The excellence factor refers to the impact made by books like *In search of excellence*,[12] in which Peters and Waterman noted that the excellent companies were people-orientated and ran a wide range of 'people programmes'. The Japanese connection was summed up in works like *The art of Japanese management* by Pascale and Athos[13] and *Theory Z* by Ouchi.[14] These studied the secret of Japanese success, attributing much of it to the creation of powerful organization cultures from which are derived shared values between managements which emphasize mutuality.

Further contributions to the development of HRM came from the combined effects of the enterprise culture and the changing context of management as described in Chapter 1. But these factors have had a greater impact

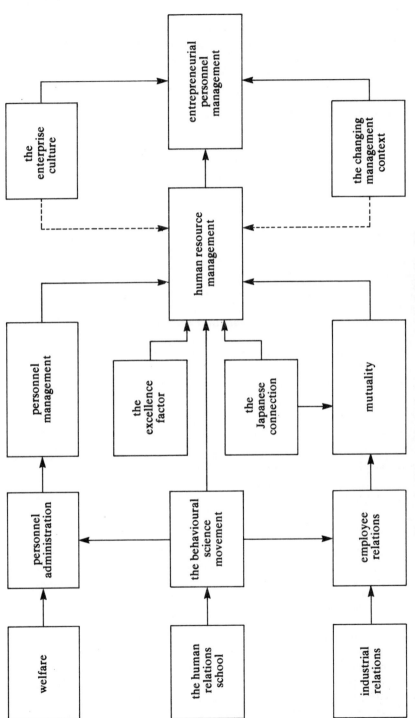

Figure 2.1 Personnel management: a model of the changing scene

on the development of the entrepreneurial performance-based approach to personnel management with its emphasis on achieving competitive advantage, added value, innovation and, in Rosabeth Moss Kanter's words, 'a culture of pride and a climate of success'.[15]

The HRM and entrepreneurial approaches are both concerned with the impact of the personnel function on the bottom line and are closely linked. But they are sufficiently different to justify the separate descriptions of them contained in the next two sections of this chapter.

HUMAN RESOURCE MANAGEMENT

HRM is a strategic approach to the acquisition, motivation, development and management of the organization's human resources. Its programmes need to be relevant to the organization's circumstances: its purpose, its technology and methods of working, the environment in which it operates, its dynamics (rate of growth or change), the type of people it employs and its industrial relations situation (the presence and strength of trade unions). HRM policies and activities are linked closely with corporate strategy and must fit the culture of the oganization.

HRM is based on four fundamental principles:

1   Human resources are the most important assets of an organization, and their effective management is the key to its success.

2   This success is most likely to be achieved if the personnel policies and procedures of the enterprise are closely linked with and make a major contribution to the achievement of corporate objectives and strategic plans.

3   The corporate culture and the values, organizational climate and managerial behaviour that emanate from that culture will exert a major influence on the achievement of excellence. This culture must therefore be managed, which means that organizational values may need to be changed or reinforced, and continuous effort, starting from the top, may be required to get them accepted and acted upon.

4   Integration, in the sense of getting the members of the organization working together with a sense of common purpose, is an important aim of HRM, but this must take account of the fact that all organizations are pluralist societies in which people have differing interests and concerns which they may well feel need to be defended collectively.

Paul Miller has emphasized the strategic nature of HRM which 'encompasses those decisions and actions which concern the management and employees *at all levels* in the business'.[16] He has suggested that 'if managements manage their employees in ways which recognize their role in strategy implementation, it is behaving strategically.'

A system of HRM is without question designed, maintained and utilized primarily for the benefit of the organization. Research in the United States indicated that the characteristics of companies such as Cummins Engine, General Foods, Hewlett Packard, IBM, Proctor and Gamble and Texas Instruments which have adopted the HRM approach on this basis are:

1   They are conspicuously well managed and have consistently achieved high levels of performance and earnings.

2   They are innovative in other fields as well, so that their interest in HRM is part of a long-term commitment to advanced management practices.

3   Decisions to implement HRM are made at top management level and are expressed in policy which works downwards into organizations through structural change.

4   There is a preoccupation with the nature of work itself – reorganizing and restructuring line functions and the jobs of the people working in these functions.

THE ENTREPRENEURIAL MODEL

The entrepreneurial approach starts with the premise that human resource activities have a major impact on individual performance and hence on productivity and organizational performance. It is market-orientated and always aware that the business and the people who work in it must be flexible, must be capable of responding quickly to exploit opportunities and must create and maintain market momentum. It is innovative, concerning itself with keeping the business at the forefront in the fields of market and product development and in the use of new technology. It is aware that the cutting edge for change must be wielded by people who have the will and the competences to 'seize the day' and to make things happen. It is equally aware that organizations must deliberately maintain programmes of continuous renewal.

Finally, those who adopt the entrepreneurial approach know that the organization exists to deliver value to its customers. They know that the management team, of which the personnel manager is a key member, is there to create that added value through effective human asset investment and management and a constant drive to improve business performance as measured ultimately by the bottom line.

This entrepreneurial model forms the background for the rest of the book, beginning with a description of how it was applied in Book Club Associates and continuing in the next chapter with an analysis of the drive towards an entrepreneurial approach to personnel management.

The BCA experience

Book Club Associates is a young, highly successful firm which is a dominant force in its market. Its success can be largely attributed to its culture, values and management style. Suitable adjectives with which to describe the way things are done in BCA are opportunistic, entrepreneurial, dynamic and informal. It believes in achieving a high degree of professionalism in the things that count – marketing and the provision and management of its key resources, finance, operational systems, information technology and people. The climate is friendly. There are, of course, disagreements on business matters, but they are dealt with openly and not on a personal basis.

Management style is informal, with a tendency towards the autocratic – a function of the type of business BCA is in, where quick reactions and fast decisions are a way of life. Informal channels of communications work well, but BCA has not been particularly good at developing formal systems. Integration, when there are a lot of 'intrapreneurs' (entrepreneurs operating within the company) about, is a continuing problem. For many years BCA has used cross-departmental project teams to look at corporate marketing developments, but more could be done.

Another important aim is to preserve what is good about the culture and not to indulge in change for change's sake. In BCA's case, this means deliberately promoting a climate of enterprise, endeavour and informality, resisting pressures for excessive bureaucracy, flattening the organization structure wherever possible to compress hierarchies, and continuing to encourage a joint approach to planning and problem-solving. This is done by senior management setting an example, by specific organizational methods, including the extensive use of project teams, and by group training designed to develop skills in working with and leading teams.

The continuous analysis of the impact of the culture on organizational behaviour is used as the basis for planning change programmes – in BCA's case opening up communications – and for achieving more participation through quality circles and other means.

This approach has worked well in BCA although there is nothing particularly special about it. How it can work elsewhere is discussed in the next chapter.

References

1   GILDER, George. *The spirit of enterprise*. New York, Simon and Schuster, 1984

2   PETERS, Tom *and* WATERMAN, Robert. *In search of excellence*. New York, Harper and Row, 1982

3   COWAN, Nick. 'Change and the personnel profession'. *Personnel Management*. January, 1988. pp 32–36

4   ARMSTRONG, Michael. 'Human resource management: a case of the emperor's new clothes'. *Personnel Management*, August 1987. pp 30–35

5   WALTON, Richard. 'From control to commitment in the work place'. *Harvard Business Review*, March–April, 1985. pp 77–84

6   KANTER, Rosabeth Moss. *The change masters*. London, Allen & Unwin, 1984

7   HENDRY, Chris, PETTIGREW, Andrew *and* SPARROW, Paul. 'Changing patterns of human resource management'. *Personnel Management*. November 1988, pp 37–41

8   BEER, Michael *and* SPECTOR, Bert. 'Transformations in HR Management'. *HRM Trends and Challenges* (ed. WALTON, Richard and LAWRENCE, Paul). Boston, Harvard Business School Press, 1985

9   PETERS, Tom *and* AUSTIN, Nancy. *A passion for excellence*. London, Collins, 1985

10 GUEST, David. 'Personnel and HRM – can you tell the difference?' *Personnel Management*, January 1989, pp 48–51

11 TYSON, Shaun *and* FELL, Alan. *Evaluating the personnel function*. London, Hutchinson, 1986

12 PETERS *and* WATERMAN. *op. cit.*

13 PASCALE, Richard *and* ATHOS, Anthony. *The art of Japanese management*. New York, Simon & Schuster, 1981

14 OUCHI, William. *Theory Z*. Reading, Mass., Addison-Wesley, 1981

15 KANTER. *op. cit.*

16 MILLER, Paul. 'Strategic personnel management: what it is and what it isn't'. *Personnel Management*, February, 1989 pp 46–51

3 The Entrepreneurial Personnel Function

An entrepreneurial personnel function will have objectives developed from and integrated with the needs of the business as expressed by its mission statement, its strategic plans and its programmes for achieving corporate goals. The members of the function should be expected to carry out their roles in accordance with these objectives, but in the context of an environment in which personnel management is to a large extent a support function.

Personnel managers can contribute significantly to the bottom line but usually by indirect means. They are enablers, but enablers with a sense of purpose. That purpose is furthering the achievement of business goals by the effective procurement, development and motivation of the resource which is instrumental in attaining these goals – the people employed in the enterprise.

Against this background, this chapter explores:

1 the overall concept of personnel management as an enabling function which, however, is, or should be, very much involved in the formulation and implementation of corporate strategies;

2 the variations inevitably imposed on this concept by the environment in which the organization operates, its culture, purposes and technology;

3 the main areas on which entrepreneurial personnel managers must focus their attention: performance, change, integration, management processes and the value set of the enterprise;

4 the objectives that entrepreneurial personnel managers set for themselves and their departments;

5 the basis upon which an entrepreneurial personnel department should be organized (Chapter 4 discusses how such a department should be staffed).

OVERALL DEFINITION

Len Peach defined personnel management as follows:

> Personnel management is concerned with creating an environ-
> ment which enables line management to recruit, train and moti-
> vate the people they need for today's and tomorrow's jobs. In
> other words, personnel management is an enabling function
> which creates a particular set of policies, but line managers are
> directly responsible for the people they control.
>
> If you accept that line managers mean it when they agree with
> you that human effort is the most important part of their enter-
> prise, that it makes the difference between success and failure,
> then it must be our job to focus on the human assets. This
> involves making sure that people of the right calibre are
> recruited and retained by the organization. However, the dan-
> gers are that this focuses on the immediate so that personnel
> managers finish up as short-term operators. This is why I come
> back to my definition of creating an environment. In my view,
> personnel management has to be an essential part of the long-
> term strategic planning of an organization.

VARIATIONS IN THE ROLE

Before considering within the context of this overall definition how the role
of personnel management is changing, the point needs to be made that there
are considerable variations in the work of the personnel department. Nick
Cowan said that:

> I always see personnel management as operating at three levels:
> at the basic level it is about fundamental employment matters –
> selecting people, paying them and telling them what to do; at the
> next level, personnel management gets into systems – manpower
> planning, performance appraisal, job evaluation, that sort of
> thing; at the highest level, personnel management is into the
> business of maximizing the effectiveness of people: resourcing in
> the widest sense, training and development. Then you really
> begin to need professional expertise and knowledge, and it's not
> something that anyone can do. It's at this level that the personnel
> manager really gets incorporated into the business – through
> involvement with management development and customer care
> programmes.

Len Peach suggested that: 'The role will vary according to the particular
circumstances in which one finds oneself.' This means that it is only possible
to generalize about trends, although the generalizations that follow in this

chapter are based on a fair degree of concensus amongst the personnel directors interviewed for this book.

Peter Hobbs amplified Len Peach's comments when he said of the role of the personnel function:

> It is critically dependent on the situation – the structure and mode of operation of the organization and the differences that exist between centralized and decentralized operators. The ideal situation is where one has a board which works as a team and a chief executive who understands that the people end of the business represents an investment infinitely greater than the technology he has on the ground. The need is, first, for a real interest and feeling for trust, getting the best from existing people, secondly ensuring that sufficient well trained and properly motivated people are in the pipeline to succeed whoever is already there to meet perceived future business needs and, thirdly, being genuinely sympathetic to the whole business of motivating and leading people in an organization.

THE ENTREPRENEURIAL FOCUS

When addressing this need and defining their objectives, personnel directors and managers should focus their attention on five main areas: performance, change, momentum, integration, and the development of management processes. These objectives need to be defined within the context of the entrepreneurial nature of personnel work and in terms of what the personnel function is there to achieve, and the function must be organized and staffed appropriately.

Performance

Personnel people exist to help create a climate of success in which high levels of performance are reached. They have to ensure that the human resources required by the organization to meet these demands are available and developed to achieve their full potential. Don Young was in no doubt as Group Personnel Director of Thorn EMI that he could and should make a major contribution to turning round the company when it was going through a period of recession in the early 1980s (from which the firm has by now more than fully recovered). He submitted a paper to the main board titled 'The strategic development of organization and management' which, under the heading 'Putting the house in order', outlined a first phase, the major focal points of which were:

1   Constructing an organization which would address the main causes of operational and competitive performance;

2   Assessing the quality and performance of the key managers in the business units;

3   Reviewing those managers who are not capable of performing to standard and removing them;

4   Restructuring most of the business and devolving responsibility and accountability, within a strong strategic and financial control framework;

5   Developing planning and control systems which would enable performance to be managed.

During phase two of this development programme the focus as proposed by Young was concentrated on:

1   Developing strategic management capability in the major SBU's (strategic business units);

2   Putting in place managements and organizations which can manage international business development rather than short-term performance improvement and turnround.

3   Changing the shape and functioning of the company organization to match the evolving strategic shape of the business;

4   Developing strength in depth.

The final stage was concerned with developing durable businesses and organizations with the emphasis on:

1   Recruitment and placement of a regular stream of high-quality younger managers and potential managers;

2   Internationalization of management and the development of international management skills.

3   Development of stable and distinctive philosophies in performance management, compensation and management development.

4   Movement of managers between the various parts of the company for business and career development purposes.

5   Company-based management training, with adequate training being an entry qualification for jobs.

In Book Club Associates the human resource section of the corporate plan became, in effect, a performance plan with proposals for deliberately promoting 'a climate of enterprise and endeavour'. The proposals were prefaced by the following remarks:

> BCA is a successful business. It must be kept that way. There is no secret to our success. It has been achieved solely by the people we employ and the way in which they have been organized and managed. But it could be said that this success is partly

fortuitous. And in the face of the changes and turbulence ahead of us we cannot afford to rely on chance. Our future is utterly dependent on having an explicit and coherent strategy for developing and maintaining the highest standards of performance.

The recommendations that followed were for a performance management programme which set out plans (which have since been progressively implemented) for:

(a)   increasing the accountability of managers for results;

(b)   relating pay more specifically to performance;

(c)   increasing commitment by better communications, more involvement of employees in the affairs of the firm and by comprehensive programmes of performance-related training, i.e. training which would be action-orientated towards specific and measurable improvements.

This emphasis on performance means that the personnel function has to be seen as a part of the business. Rhiannon Chapman put this point well when she said:

I actually believe quite strongly that the personnel function has little case for existing on its own merits at all. Unless the personnel function is seen to be making a real added-value contribution to the organization then it has no merit, no justification for existing. And that is a message that very few personnel managers seem to take on board. Many personnel people have had very little exposure to business problems, which is why, of course, they are very vulnerable when the business comes under pressure. The personnel function should be quite visibly part of the business process as a management function, not just as a professional support function, although of course there are strong elements of that. And it certainly isn't just an administrative function.

Change

Geoff Armstrong is clear that:

The role of the personnel function is to bring about change and to create a climate within which effective contributions can be made. Managers should be encouraged to think boldly and to think in an unfettered way. The personnel function should then enable them to achieve what they have been bold enough to think.

And at the Cadbury Schweppes international personnel conference the comment was made that:

It is in the end fruitless to disentangle the contributions of the personnel function from those of general managers and colleagues in other parts of the business. A cultural change has, however, been taking place. It has been showing in the Group's results, and personnel managers have played a pro-active and successful part in it. . . . The task remains, without complacency, both to do better the things that the function is already doing and to take on board new opportunities and challenges. Competition has not stood still in the management of people either, and personnel managers have to work even harder in a still tougher environment to maintain a competitive advantage.

Nick Cowan has made the point that:

Over the past 75 years personnel management has changed radically. Technically, the profession would be unrecognizable to those who pioneered it. As personnel managers have become more competent technically, the emphasis has moved towards questions of performance and evaluation.[1]

He also noted that there had been a shift in emphasis in the profession 'from technician to business manager, a vital change' and, importantly, that: 'As the rate of change increases personnel management will increasingly be concerned with implementing change, whether in skill development, attitude change or cultural accommodation.'

Momentum

Personnel management, according to Jeff Roberts, is:

Changing from its traditional bureaucratic role, which is almost a policeman role – with a procedures manual which is a foot thick – to becoming a much more pro-active function.

Purely reactive personnel managers will not survive long in the fast-moving business of today. They have to play an active part in the dynamic processes of the organization. They must know where the business is going and what must be done to get there. They have to do everything they can to ensure that the momentum for growth and success is sustained.

The focus on momentum was highlighted by John Hougham as follows:

If I had to say in a couple of words what I think we are all about in this business today, it's 'maintaining momentum'. We've got a very good momentum going in this company (Ford), a momentum for change, a momentum for co-operation involving employees. And I think what the company is looking for us (the personnel function) to do is to maintain that momentum.

Perhaps not to do anything very much more dramatic. I think that we are heading in the right direction. There aren't very many more dramas that I can see in the immediate future, like the changes of 1985. We know where we are going, we know what we have to do to get there, we are pretty sure we are on the right course, and what we have to do now is to keep that momentum going.

Integration

Terry Murphy expressed his view that the personnel function should be interwoven into the business fabric as follows:

> It's my belief, that the only way in which the personnel function can operate effectively and contribute to the bottom line is if the personnel director is (a) integrated with the rest of the business planning team, and (b) has got the capability of taking the business plans and converting them to sensible long-term manpower or human resource plans. What you want, in fact, is to have a match between what you have planned for the resourcing activity and the actual business development activity. So that is where I started from and I guess I put that together as a result of seeing how personnel operated some years ago in Marconi, where the function itself was fairly sophisticated but was in almost every way divorced from the business plan. It was seen as something in a little compartment on its own dealing with the nasty things that line management didn't want to deal with such as industrial relations, pay rates, job evaluation, and so on and so forth.

The reference here to the importance of linking business and human resource planning was echoed by a number of the personnel directors interviewed during the course of preparing this book. They referred frequently to strategic planning as an integrative process in itself and to the importance of the personnel function's full involvement as a means of contributing to the bottom line. This was recognized in a special way at Book Club Associates where the writer, as personnel director, was also responsible for the preparation of the corporate plan for the business as a whole.

John Hougham, for example, referred to the 'integrated web' of personnel activities linked to the business plan such as 'organization structuring, resourcing, identifying potential, appraising performance and relating appraisals to pay'. The Ford planning process, no part of which stands in isolation, says:

> These are the issues which sales and marketing have highlighted, these are the issues which manufacturing has highlighted and these are the things which we think that in personnel we ought to be doing to respond to these requirements and, by the way, here are some ideas of our own.

Management processes

The personnel function has increasingly to pay attention to the management processes required to improve bottom-line results. A systems approach is required. Systems take something from the environment called an input, change it through a process and then release the changed item back into the environment as an output. Effective systems establish goals or objectives towards which they process the input, plus a feedback mechanism to keep them on track. In personnel terms, people are inputs to the organizational system: to be resourced, developed and motivated so that defined outputs expressed as goals or objectives are achieved. This process is continuously guided and monitored by members of the personnel function to ensure that it is operating effectively.

Don Young feels strongly that personnel issues are very much concerned with this process and its impact on performance. He believes that the personnel function must help to 'build a process which has coherence in the sense of what the organization should be doing over a period of time'. In his view, the planning system has a major role in the management process and needs to be shaped 'as a means of sending messages to the organization on what management values and what management wants people to pay attention to'. But he advised against setting up corporate systems in too big a way: 'The energy needed at the centre to maintain systems in place becomes a hangman's noose, if you get too involved.'

Don Beattie suggested that 'there are going to be some elements of process in any personnel director's tool kit.' He defined it as the standards that are adopted in organizations for carrying out certain operational tasks. Process is not simply about procedures, which could vary from part to part of a company, nor policies 'within which individual line managers have significant scope to do their own thing but which define lines to achieve the outputs or objectives required'. Don Beattie gave the example of manpower planning:

> How do we do manpower planning? Do we express our manpower plans in 101 different ways or do we indicate: 'That's the way we want the manpower plan to look when it's finished'? What, in effect, we *do* say is that 'We are not going to do manpower planning for you at the centre, but, believe you me, like an aspirin a day, doing manpower planning *this way* is good for you. So please take it on board and use it as a tool of the business. And if you want to convince me, line director, line personnel director, that this is not good for your business, I will consider changing it, but look forward to an interesting discussion.' There should be very few of these process things, but they should be the absolute pillars of running an organization.

Guidelines from the centre on processes are required but everyone would agree with Don Beattie that they should not be overdone. If decentralization is going to work, managers at local levels must be able to make their own decisions within the framework of broad corporate guidelines. In this connection, Peter Hobbs suggests that:

> In the personnel field, if you do a few things really well then the organization is going to keep going. Things like defining jobs adequately, recruiting people who fit requirements and rewarding them consistently – like if they do well they get more and if they do badly in matters within their control they get penalized. If you get these basic systems actually operating then it doesn't matter what happens to the MD or anyone else, because the organization will keep on going reasonably well along its course. Until, that is, something external happens which actually deprives it of its ability or desire for being there in the first place.

And he added a word of caution to those who try too hard to impose process from the centre:

> If anyone starts off with the belief that they are going to be able in any organization to get everyone to do the same thing at the same time to the same level of excellence, then they are crazy. All we can do is have something like a general approach.

The traditional role

Not everything has changed. The personnel department is still a support function, providing efficient and cost-effective resourcing, training and pay administration services, running an occupational health service, administering personnel procedure, maintaining computerized personnel information systems, handling grievances, disciplinary matters and personal problems, managing communications and consultative processes and ensuring that the legal obligations of the company are met. As Peter Hobbs said:

> We are a support function; we are enablers. We may often present managers with some of the stars in the firmament and say 'Hey, isn't that nice' and get people to reach for them. But we are enabling other people to do things rather than doing things ourselves.

Values

Acting as a support function in a hard-nosed entrepreneurial environment does not, however, mean that personnel managers can remain unconcerned about maintaining and operating within the core values of the organization. The value set of an enterprise will consist of the accepted beliefs on what is best or good for the organization and what should or should not happen. Values express what management believes to be important and define how it intends to conduct the business and to treat the people who work in it. So far as people are concerned, the core values will cover dealing with them fairly (equity), providing equal opportunities for all, using the principles of natural justice when handling disciplinary matters, responding to real or even imaginary grievances seriously and with consideration, creating and maintaining a safe and healthy working environment, exercising continuous concern over the quality of working life and providing the maximum amount of security of employment consistent with meeting what may sometimes have to be regarded as overriding organizational needs. The organization does not exist simply for the people it employs but neither can it exist in spite of them.

There will be times when the responsibilities of the organization to its various stake holders will have to be exercised at the expense of one or other of them. Health and safety programmes and improvements in working conditions will quite justifiably take money off the bottom line. It can be argued that they are investments which will pay off by creating a more contented and, presumably, a more committed workforce. But this is not the reason for launching such programmes. Individuals can suffer because organizations have to do things for the good of the whole at the expense of some of the parts, especially when they are under external pressure. Redundancies are sometimes unavoidable, prospects may be restricted, people may stagnate in dead-end jobs and managers may 'plateau out' in their forties and become frustrated.

Personnel managers cannot always prevent these things happening but they can try to alleviate the pain. They can make strenuous efforts to avoid redundancies by re-training, re-deployment or freezing recruitment in good time. If, to use an awful American expression, 'down-sizing' has to happen, then they can, to use another Americanism, at least launch 'outplacement' programmes to find new jobs for those affected. They can create re-training opportunities and look at the scope for job enrichment.

Personnel managers should be aware of the implications of the introduction of new technology and provide advice on how it should be managed to minimize disruption and detrimental effects on the people concerned. And this includes not only the possibility of job losses but also the health and safety implications of new plant, equipment and methods. For example, they can press for ergonomic factors to be taken into account in designing a new work system so as to minimize the possibility of repetitive strain injury.

Flexibility implies multi-skilling and personnel managers need to launch and maintain training programmes which will help people to cope with the new demands made upon them.

Organizational and individual needs
In 1986 Mackay and Torrington claimed that:

> Personnel management is never identified with management interests as it becomes ineffective when not able to understand and articulate the aspirations of the workforce.[2]

Not everyone would accept this claim. Personnel managers should indeed be concerned with the aspirations of the workforce, but they cannot let that concern operate against the interests of the organization as a whole so long as those interests in general coincide with those of its members. Personnel managers cannot set themselves up as the sole conscience of the organization, but they can act as guardians of its values. It is their right and duty to point out if any proposed action is inconsistent with those values. As Len Peach put it:

> Personnel directors are the guardians of the personnel tenets of the organization and if there is an appeal then it is their job to ensure that the appeal is fairly heard. They guard the process. But they also guard the equity and the fairness of the system as well.

Entrepreneurial personnel directors and managers will sometimes be placed in a dilemma when balancing the rights of individuals against the needs of the organization. Rhiannon Chapman commented on this problem as follows:

> I have frequently found myself in the situation where the interests of the individual are so different from the interests of the organization that to arrive at an objective and helpful view is quite tricky. For whatever reason, one has a natural anathema to putting the business first irrespective of the claims of the individual. But from a business point of view, how much more investment can be justified being made in that individual? How much of my time should be spent trying to find a better place for an individual in the organization when there are perhaps 500 other people who are in a way more deserving of my time and attention and, if I gave them that attention, the busines would be getting a better return on my efforts? That's the dilemma and I think it's the sort of dilemma that a lot of personnel people are more conscious of a lot of their time than I can be. Which is why they are not comfortable taking the business perspective.

Objectives

To play their full part in helping the organization to achieve its business objectives, personnel directors and managers have to be quite clear about the objectives of the personnel function and their own objectives within the function. The starting point in the thinking of personnel people, according to Mike Stanton, should be to ask the questions: What is this organization for? What are its objectives? And what part can the effective management of people play in achieving those objectives?

In the light of the answers to the above questions, the routes to success can be mapped out under these headings:

● creating an organization which fits the marketing environment and management style of the firm, is relevant to its purpose and technology and makes the best uses of the skills and abilities of its members.

- building a culture and climate which encourages commitment.
- formulating resourcing and reward strategies which attract, retain and motivate the people required by the organization.
- focusing on quality through people.
- developing employees' competences in order to respond quickly and flexibly to marketing opportunities and to build and maintain competitive advantage.

Every organization is different and will therefore produce different answers to Mike Stanton's questions and plan different routes to success. The following are some examples of statements of objectives and priorities:

Book Club Associates

In Book Club Associates the overriding objective of the personnel department was:

> To make an effective contribution to the achievement of the objectives of the firm and to the fulfilment of its social responsibilities.

This was broken down into four sub-objectives:

1   To design and develop an effective organization which will maintain BCA's competitive advantage and respond vigorously to change.
2   To obtain and develop the quality and quantity of human resources required by the organization and to help ensure that corporate goals for the added value arising from their efforts are achieved.
3   To increase the commitment of all employees to organizational objectives by sharing with them the vision for the future defined for the firm and involving them in the decisions that affect them.
4   To ensure that the core values of the firm for quality, customer service and relationships with employees are understood and acted upon and that the firm's social responsibilities are fulfilled.

Cadbury Schweppes

At Cadbury Schweppes the priorities for the personnel function were expressed by Peter Reay as:

(a)   To concentrate increased attention on appointments, deployment and redeployment so that people placed in senior positions are those who can carry through the group's growth plans, and are effectively supported, developed, motivated and rewarded. In many ways this issue of the quality of our human resources and the way they are used is the key to everything else.

(b) To ensure that personnel management is sensitive to the changing environment, understands and interprets it accurately, and as necessary triumphs over it. Technological change is perhaps the most obvious externally generated force, but the impact of educational, social and political change increases steadily, occasionally threatens the way that the group wants to manage its people and has as far as possible to be harnessed to our advantage.

(c) To build further the commitment of our employees at all levels, not least junior and middle management, to the aims of the business and to the changes which will continue to be necessary for it to prosper in the face of fierce competition. This affects particularly our employee relations strategy, but it has major implications for the quality of communications and training.

(d) To set increasingly high standards for ourselves and for all the staff who work in the personnel function. We shall have to look constantly at the function's professionalism, at its effectiveness and, in so far as it affects the latter, at its image. We are a great deal more than just a service function, but since much of the work is that which the line has given us to do, we need assume no God-given right to exist, and we have constantly to earn the right to be heard. We need to continue to take every chance to unload the less significant administrative activities, but we and our colleagues should not underestimate the quality and scale of resources needed to carry out our very demanding change objectives.

To complement these priorities, the following objectives were set for Cadbury Schweppes in the area of employee involvement:

• Produce the highest quality product at the lowest cost in line with the changing business and market conditions, and ensuring a continuing competitive advantage.

• Explore, evaluate and capitalize each distribution manpower opportunity while continuing to operate the most cost-effective system which sustains long-term growth.

• Develop the employee business link through the establishment of open communication systems that ensure employees understand and are committed to the business goals and performance.

• Create and maintain an environment which develops and nurtures long-term employee commitment.

• Develop an organization which encourages a participative management style.

• Provide direction and support to employee groups that enables those groups to initiate, adapt and accept new ideas and technology for continued profitable business growth.

• Develop a management profile that encourages a participative leadership style that embraces the organization's values and continues to improve overall company performance.

Shell UK Oil

At Shell UK Oil the personnel objectives were defined as:

> To ensure that the company's strong human resource base is used to competitive advantage by establishing a climate which demands and appropriately rewards excellence from staff and which encourages individual growth, respect, initiative and commitment, in an organization with clear roles and accountabilities.

The International Stock Exchange

The mission statement produced by the Human Resource Management Group in 1988 was:

> To develop and promote the highest quality personnel and human resource practices and initiatives in an ethical, cost-effective and timely manner to support the current and future business objectives of the International Stock Exchange (ISE) and The Securities Association (TSA) and to enable line managers to maximize the calibre, effectiveness and development of their human resources.

The personnel team at the International Stock Exchange responsible for the Central Services and Regulatory Departments (CSRD) produced the following list of action priorities:

1 To build a cohesive, effective and influential team which is business-aware and has a good understanding of human resourcing strategy and its relevance to the client's operating activities.

2 To meet specific resourcing needs whilst ensuring appropriate consistency and integration with International Stock Exchange employment practices.

3 To develop an innovative, efficient and cost-effective recruitment service which is responsive to fluctuations in business needs and forms an integral part of the corporate recruitment effort.

4 To ensure appropriate skills availability and organizational structures to meet business requirements by initiating and promoting the process

of career development to form the basis of future succession planning.

5   To encourage line managment to promote, develop and recruit staff internally within the organization and actively to participate in trainee development programmes as a means of developing both specialist and generalist skills for the future.

6   To contribute to the development of an effective staff appraisal system and to encourage its acceptance and utilization within the differing management cultures of the various client areas, identifying the benefits to be derived through clear objective setting and its association with financial objectives.

7   To contribute to the development of the personnel records system whilst preparing for the introduction of new technology, ensuring both the security and accuracy of personnel data, successful systems implementation and ongoing review of CSRD team requirements.

8   To consider immediate, medium- and long-term requirements for comprehensive management information and the provision of data to the line in order to highlight internal relativities and areas for concern and attention.

9   To support line management in the redeployment of staff in the transition period post 'A' day and in meeting the resourcing implications of the Securities and Investments Board (SIB) requirements.

10 To review and develop the merit assessment scheme for the unionized groups and extend the scheme to the remaining groups on the service incremental system, introducing appropriate salary scales with due regard to 'equal value, equal pay'.

11 To establish and develop a personnel service to the marketing directorate.

12 To assist in the development of a unified markets division, encouraging where appropriate common approaches to human resource planning and identifying opportunities for effective divisional utilization and development of resources.

13 Actively to support and develop close links with the staff consultation process and the union representation.

CARRYING OUT THE ROLE

While it is quite clear that in future the work and interests of personnel managers will have to become more closely linked to the strategic objectives of the business they serve, it is still necessary to consider how best their departments can be organized to fulfil their support role.

Peter Wickens illustrated how his personnel department functioned as follows:

The whole of the way we recruit is determined by the personnel department. They run it, administer it and are involved at every stage in it. But what we do find is that we could not now in personnel make a selection decision. If we tried we'd have a riot amongst our managers and supervisors.

Another example is our appraisal and salary progression system. The personnel department is, I guess, the owner of that system. We designed the appraisal system, we determined how frequently people should be appraised, what the structure of those appraisal meetings should be and how the rate of progression along the salary range is determined. We organize and administer the system and we will give advice and deal with problems but the actual implementation of the system is the line manager's responsibility. . . . Our task is to create the environment, set the framework and equip people to work within that framework. But it is not our task to say 'look you've failed on your job, we'll come down and fix your problem for you'.

Decentralization

The thrust in recent years has been to decentralize, so that the corporate personnel department is left with the minimum of staff and a role which concentrates on overall business and organizational considerations: the appointment, development and remuneration of the group's senior managers, the formulation of process and policy guidelines and the monitoring of the application of these guidelines at divisional level. The group personnel director may also be involved in the appointment of subsidiary personnel directors and in reviewing their performance.

At BAT Industries the centre develops guidelines which suggest standards and methodology but they are not worked out in fine detail. John Crosby gave the following example in the field of remuneration:

We say to companies that they must have a job evaluation structure but we don't say which method. That's their choice. We also say that when they carry out salary surveys they should have at least two ways of looking at the market. One, ideally, would be job matching which is very much first-hand stuff conducted personally with comparative companies outside. The second method would be to take part in a larger consultant's survey which would allow them to see how they compare against a large number of companies.

Peter Reay had the following comments to make on the trend towards decentralization:

What's going to happen in a business like ours or anybody else's is that because of information technology and for other reasons,

you'll increasingly get a kind of policy control central oganization with much greater decentralization into smaller units
which are market sensitive. What you will get at each of these
local business units is a relatively small team of people who
really do have to work together to exploit the market they are in.
Wherever we've got people on the management team in that
kind of situation, my judgement is that they attend the meetings,
they contribute the ideas, they share in the direction and they
share in the achievement of profit targets.

At Legal and General John Skae said that, following their own work and a
consultant's study, it was decided that:

It would be correct to go into strategic business units, to devolve
the running of the business and give the responsibility for all
aspects of a business unit to the top guy. So we moved the
accountants out and we moved the systems analysts and pro-
grammers out into each unit. So it was natural to decentralize the
personnel department too. . . . The dead hand of personnel,
which was part of the old hierarchical administrative system, no
longer exists.

The Abbey National reorganization

Terry Murphy explained his broad philosophy of what the personnel or
human resource function is about:

I had a vision which developed, I suppose, over about 15 years,
of a function which was interwoven into the fabric of the
business and was not itself differentiated into a series of
sub-functions. I have too often seen the personnel function
fragmented into industrial relations, training, recruitment and
selection, record keeping *per se* or manpower planning as a
more distinguished feature of record keeping then a projective
process.
    I had a rather different view of the personnel function. I
started on the basis of 'Look, the whole purpose of the function
is resourcing.' Whether you resource internally by developing
your existing people or resource externally by recruiting, or
whether you resource by a mixture of both is really irrelevant.
    Coupled with this you have a number of hygiene or main-
tenance functions such as maintaining good employee relations,
ensuring that people are paid the proper rate for the job depending on the marketplace, and ensuring that you have a good
computerized personnel data base and so on.
    And lastly, in order to ensure that you can resource effectively,
you have a strategic function which does the manpower

planning, the succession planning and the regular audit of resources so that you have a good picture of what you have got, which you then put against the business plan and compare with what you need. So that was how I saw the personnel function, basically as a resourcing activity. Now if this is what it is, there is no room for divisions between personnel and training, for example. They are all part of the same game.

Against this background, when he joined Abbey National in 1980, Terry Murphy found all sorts of divisions and sub-divisions at headquarters:

For example, in the management development area I discovered that there was a group who were running management assessment centres who were also doing some work on appraisals. There was another group in management development doing appraisal training and also devising some thoughts on appraisal. And there was yet another group in personnel who were also developing thoughts on appraisals, but none of them knew that the others were doing it! So the first thing I had to do there was to totally integrate personnel and training, get them thinking along the same lines and get them thinking along the lines of resourcing more than anything else.

Centralization also caused problems:

When I joined Abbey National in 1980, I found there was a centralized bureaucracy trying to run a national personnel service from one location in London. So it meant in effect that if a branch manager in Aberdeen wanted to recruit someone he could get as far as the interview but then all the paperwork had to be sent to London for processing and all the references were taken up and all the offers were dealt with from London. Now I failed to see when I arrived how somebody sitting in London could deal with the local problems in Aberdeen. So I had to decentralize this massive bureaucracy and put regional personnel officers out on the ground where the action was.

Fluidity

The old rigid distinctions between a personnel department providing various administrative services and the line departments who get on and do things is beginning to be blurred. Barry Curnow's comments on this trend were:

I have a vision of personnel where there is much more movement of business people into personnel jobs and personnel people into line management jobs. We will then move towards a more integrated future where the functional distinctions between personnel and marketing, sales, line management and research really are things of the past. The matrix – the team working at the top of successful enterprises – seems to me to be all about fluidity, not about compartments and pigeonholes and lines and demarcation boxes in an organization, but about getting the chemistry right at the top of the company.

Overall trends in organizing the personnel function

The overall trends in the organization of the personnel function are as follows:

1 The function is headed by a personnel director who is part of the top management team and, as a board member, plays an equal part with his or her colleagues in formulating business strategies, monitoring performance and initiating action to exploit marketing opportunities or to take corrective action where required. At the same time, the personnel director will be analyzing and assessing strategies and business trends affecting the organization in terms of its human resources. He or she will ensure that the results of these assessments are fully taken into account in formulating corporate plans and programmes and that action is taken within the human resource area as and when required.

2 The function is decentralized into strategic business units (SBUs), which are closely related to their markets. Personnel directors and managers in these SBUs are heavily involved in creating added value from the unit's human resources which have been selected, trained, developed and rewarded to fit the particular needs of the business in its own market niche. The SBU personnel staff work within guidelines on process and policy from the centre but are left a considerable degree of freedom to interpret and apply them in accordance with local requirements.

3 The corporate personnel function exists simply to provide advice, support and services in areas which concern top management and affect the corporation as a whole, especially those concerning organizational performance, cultural change and management resources. It formulates corporate guidelines and monitors their implementation. The function comprises no more than two or three top-level people and their secretarial or administrative support staff.

4 These trends are all directed towards the improvement of the effectiveness of the personnel function as a contributor to the bottom line, but they make heavy demands on the staff in the function. It is therefore necessary to consider in greater depth the staffing implications of these developments, which will be discussed in the next chapter.

References

1 COWAN, Nick. 'Change and the personnel profession'. *Personnel Management.* January 1988, pp 32–36
2 MACKAY, L. *and* TORRINGTON, D. *The changing nature of personnel management.* London. Institute of Personnel Management, 1986

4   Staffing the Entrepreneurial Personnel Function

THE BASIC PROBLEM

Rhiannon Chapman summed up the basic problem of staffing an entrepreneurial personnel function as follows:

> Personnel people in the main go into personnel or find themselves in personnel because they have a particular disposition to be of service and to get involved in helping people and making good things happen. They are essentially implementors and operational people – that's the kick for them. And there is the sense in a lot of personnel people that the rest is mucky, whimsical, political and manipulative and all kinds of things they feel uncomfortable about because it impacts on their strong personal ethic about people and how they are deployed in organizations.
>
> So you get a lot of extremely good personnel people who actually don't want to know about the business side of things because it contains all those nasty things they don't approve of. At the same time, you get a good percentage of business people who have very low expectations of the support they will get from the personnel function and see it as purely administrative because that is the chief visible impact it makes. They do not therefore ask for high-level involvement from their personnel people. From both ends you have got people who are actually standing back from one another, so there is a lot to do to create an opportunity which will help them work together. That's the difficulty. There's not much common ground and, somehow, common ground has got to be established.

LIVING WITH AMBIGUITY

Ambiguity often has to be a way of life for personnel people. As Arthur Miller would say: 'It goes with the territory.' It arises for the reasons given by Rhiannon Chapman. In other words, partly because of the attitudes of line managers to personnel specialists and partly because the latter are unsure about where they stand, there is confusion in many personnel minds between ideals and reality. So the personnel organization has to be staffed with people who can rise above and triumph over ambiguity, or at least can learn to live with it.

This doesn't always happen, as was pointed out by Alan Fell:

> Personnel people are not necessarily keen to deal with ambiguities. They understand them but they're not always readily able to handle them. I think where personnel people are quite good is that they know that the organization is a tissue, a web of relationships, a web of IOUs, a web of deceit, a web of power-broking; a web of all these things. Where they sometimes bottle out is they can't actually get in amongst it. They can observe it. In fact they can actually be quite acute observers and therefore have a value to the chief executive because they can give an independent view of what's going on down there in the snake pit. The chief executive may actually want them there. It's a very lonely job being the chief executive and they can welcome someone who, they say to themselves, is sitting squat-legged on the rim of the snake pit and not amongst it, and maybe he's useful to me.
>
> But as rim sitters – is there such a word? – personnel people can be marginalized because they always seem to be no more than acute observers. At best they become cynical and at worst they start misusing the information. There are lots of examples of personnel people who've misused the information.

BUSINESS AWARENESS

The theme of this book is that personnel professionals should be fully aware of the needs of the business as a commercial, market-orientated and profit-making enterprise and fully aware of the contribution they can make to fulfilling those needs.

Mike Stanton is pessimistic about the availability of the kind of people required to staff the entrepreneurial personnel function:

> The proportion of senior personnel people who can talk intelligently about business economics and business strategy, who can appear to be businessmen or women first (where their priorities should be) and personnel people second, is all too small. . . . I think that the profession has a lot to do to raise its standards, to get higher quality people into it and to ensure that its members are educated generally in business as well as specifically in personnel management.

The research team at Warwick University which investigated changing patterns of human resource management pointed out that there were three core issues that personnel functions needed to address: their competency, their credibility and the need to perceive themselves as developers. The team suggested that:

> The requirement is the ability to take, and implement, a strategic view of the whole range of personnel practices in relation to business activity as a whole, and for the personnel function. There is not just an issue of developing skills but also one of needing to link together business, technical and HRM skills. . . . Our research suggests that there is, unfortunately, a shortage of people with such skills and competences within firms.[1]

WHERE DO BUSINESS-ORIENTATED PERSONNEL PEOPLE COME FROM?

Alan Fell is quite clear about this:

> If you are going to be successful at this (taking a business view) then you're going to have to actually know how to make money. Personnel has been entirely brought up operating cost centres. Some of them are very large cost centres. I mean, there must be people around with big budgets. But they're not profit centres, they are not going to make money.
>
> Now running a cost centre is fascinating and interesting and very demanding, very responsible, but it's not making money. There's no new money.

He believes that the problem occurs because too many personnel people have been isolated from the real business world:

> That I think comes from the fact that there is a whole raft of personnel people for whom the issue never arises. They never have to go out there and say 'Look Mr Armstrong, would you like to buy my widget, and Mr Armstrong says no, and there's no money coming in!'

The personnel director or manager, according to Fell, has got to be seen as:

> One of us, not there to say no or not there to say maybe, but in fact someone who says and understands that it is very cold and lonely out there. And unless you've gone out with a salesman and sat in his car on a November afternoon in Cardiff, rain pissing down, and you've made all those 'cold calls' where you can't get in, you won't realize that you have no right just to be spending money.

There seems to be a lot of doubt around on the ability of personnel people to rise to meet the new challenges. Perhaps this is why Sir Michael Edwardes could say that 'personnel management is too important to be left to personnel managers'. Tyson and Fell suggest that there is a crisis in personnel management which involves a crisis in confidence amongst personnel managers themselves and a related crisis over their credibility amongst their managerial colleagues.[2]

Alan Fell, in expressing concern about the marginalization of personnel specialists if they are not operating within the business rather than on the periphery, issued a warning about the danger of the 'Balkanization' of personnel. In his words:

> There will be a group, a vast group of personnel specialists peddling very high levels of expertise in particular aspects of personnel. They will be very task orientated, high quality, but there will not be the people around to cement the whole thing together.

WHAT'S TO BE DONE?

Barry Curnow suggested that there were three things aspiring personnel professionals should do in order to reach positions where they could participate fully in an entrepreneurial environment and help their companies achieve competitive advantage:

> Firstly they must obtain at an early age some line management experience in running things. It doesn't matter what it is, but to have run something is more important than what it is you have run. They must, moreover, have held a line job which involves delivering measurable output through managing and leading people, making the best use of physical and financial resources and demonstrating a quantifiable bottom-line output. There is no doubt in my mind that without that, the personnel manager of the future will be incomplete and will be relegated to the side lines of administration rather than the front stage of business and people development.
>
> My second piece of advice is that they must have worked internationally if they are to be effective in the global markets of the future. This means working and getting things done in companies where the management processes are not dominated by any one culture or nationality.
>
> My third piece of advice is that personnel managers should look continually to their own self-development. We are now in a world of careers in which people cannot expect companies to do their career development for them. The paternalistic approach to training and development of the 1960s and 1970s has gone. Personnel officers who are aspiring to be the personnel directors

and business managers of the future must take accountability for managing their own learning and self-development and through that they will grow.

Relevant experience and education is one way of developing business-orientated personnel professionals. The other way is through leadership from the top in the shape of the personnel directors. Their role and how they exercise it is discussed in the next chapter.

References

1 HENDRY, Chris, PETTIGREW, Andrew *and* SPARROW, Paul. 'Changing patterns of human resource management.' *Personnel Management.* November 1988
2 TYSON, Shaun *and* FELL, Alan. *Evaluating the personnel function.* London. Hutchinson, 1986

5 The Entrepreneurial Personnel Director

Entrepreneurial personnel directors are agents of change. They are enablers. They contribute to the formulation of corporate strategies as business partners. They know that their companies exist to achieve demanding objectives as expressed in bottom-line terms. They understand that this involves innovation, growth and constant pressure to maintain competitive advantage. They appreciate that the organization has to obtain added value from its human resources. They therefore recognize the key role they play in ensuring that their firms obtain and develop the people they need and do everything possible to maximize motivation and commitment.

They accept, however, that entrepreneurial activity has to take place within the context of continuing programmes aimed at improving quality and levels of customer service. They also accept that the drive for success must not be pursued at the expense of the rights of the members of the organization to consideration, fair treatment, involvement in its affairs, the opportunity to grow within the firm and a high quality of working life.

Finally, they realize that their contribution to the bottom line requires them not only to play an active part in the affairs of the business, but also to ensure that effective and efficient support is provided to management in the shape of advice and services with regard to resourcing, training, performance and reward management and the maintenance of co-operative and harmonious relationships throughout the organization.

As a generalization, the role of the personnel director could be described as containing the following main elements:

(a) participating as a member of the board in formulating corporate strategies and plans, monitoring the performance of the company and initiating action as required;

(b) ensuring that in formulating business strategies, their human resource implications are fully understood by the chief executive and fellow board members;

(c) formulating and obtaining board approval for human resource and

55

employee relations strategies which are fully integrated with agreed corporate strategies;

(d)   bringing to the attention of the chief executive and the board human resource management issues which should be incorporated in longer-term strategies or which require short-term tactical decisions;

(e)   generally advising the chief executive on matters concerning the organization of the business, the management of change, the development of corporate culture and values, the achievement of commitment and mutuality, the improvement of organizational performance through its human resources and the resourcing, development, career planning and reward of directors and other top managers;

(f)   providing advice to co-directors on organizational, resourcing and reward matters concerning their senior people;

(g)   determining the personnel processes which are required to implement corporate human resource strategies and issuing guidelines accordingly;

(h)   directing and, as necessary, co-ordinating the implementation of human resource strategies and ensuring that corporate guidelines on personnel processes are implemented consistently, having regard to local circumstances;

(i)   ensuring the availability of the quality of personnel support and advisory services needed in the organization by paying continuous attention to the resourcing and development of the personnel function, by monitoring performance and by providing the leadership and guidance required;

(j)   participating in the planning and implementation of programmes designed to improve quality, customer service or productivity.

There are, of course, as many variations on these basic themes as there are personnel directors. The emphasis on the different aspects of the role and the priorities given to them must vary widely according to the type of organization – its structure, technology, culture, history of employee relationships, the type of people it employs, the personality and special requirements and needs of the chief executive, the general requirements and needs of co-directors, the traditional role assigned to the personnel function and the competence and credibility of the personnel director.

The following is a fairly typical although not standard example of the job description of a personnel director.

Job purpose

1   To advise on strategies and policies concerning employee relations and the organization, acquisition, motivation,

reward and development of the human resources required by the firm.

2 To direct and control the personnel activities required to implement these strategies and policies.

3 To ensure that the firm meets its social and legal obligations to its employees.

Specific accountabilities

1 Participates as a member of the Executive Board in formulating corporate strategies, policies, plans and budgets and in monitoring the firm's performance.

2 Advises the chief executive and colleagues on the personnel and employee relations policies required by the firm in all areas of human resource management.

3 Formulates and implements overall human resource strategies and specific plans derived from agreed corporate strategies to ensure the human resources needed by the firm are available as required, in terms of both quality and quantity.

4 Plans and directs human resource development, performance management and career management programmes designed to improve individual and organizational effectiveness and to give employees the best opportunities to develop their abilities and careers in the firm.

5 Develops reward management and remuneration (including pensions) policies and systems which effectively attract, retain and motivate staff, are internally equitable as well as externally competitive and operate cost-effectively.

6 Advises on employee relations strategies and policies designed to maximize involvement and commitment while minimizing conflict and, in this connection:

   (a) determines negotiating tactics within the context of agreed strategies;

   (b) leads or takes part in negotiations as required;

   (c) deals with major employee relations issues as they arise.

7 Directs the implementation of the firm's communications and staff involvement programmes – for example, quality circles, team briefing and company newsletters or bulletins.

The best way of understanding the entrepreneurial role of the personnel director, however, is to look at it from the point of view of the practitioners.

Don Beattie – STC

Don Beattie has invented the mnemonic APPLES to define what a corporate personnel function and therefore a personnel director does. This comprises:

- Audit – the function of auditing the implementation of policy and process.

- Policy – which goes hand-in-hand with audit, because if there are policies they have to be audited, and they must be written in a way which makes them capable of being audited. Policies provide the framework within which individual managers have ample scope 'to do their own thing'. They spell out the parameters for action and the limits beyond which the organization will not allow managers to go. Policies will define the fundamental beliefs which determine how the business is conducted.

- Process – which defines the standards used by managers down the line in carrying out the function. For example, a process requirement laid down at the centre may be that a common job evaluation points scheme should be used.

- Leadership – the guidance provided from the centre which ensures that the personnel function down the line works with it in ensuring 'certain key deliverables that have to permeate all parts of the company'.

- Expertise – expertise or 'expert consultancy' has to be provided at the centre but it must also be available at every level in the organization.

- Service – which consists of any service elements of the function such as pensions which have to be controlled and administered centrally or which, because of economies of scale, it would be uneconomic to devolve to subsidiary companies.

Referring to the particular role of the personnel director, Don Beattie believes there is an element of acting as the conscience of the chief executive and there is certainly a duty to 'try to catalyze the thinking of the chief executive and the key opinion formers'. Personnel directors are paid 'to know what business they are in, to know where it is going and to ensure that the input to get there is available from a human resourcing and organizational capability point of view.'

Ensuring that the personnel department functions effectively is clearly an important responsibility of the personnel director: 'My role is to set certain key result areas from the centre which define functional competence requirements down the line.'

The performance of the personnel function is monitored by Don Beattie through operational personnel reviews held about every four months. These take place with a structured agenda which reviews the objectives of members of the function and what they are actually doing. The aims are to establish that personnel people are focused on the right things, to find out 'if they've got any road blocks which are bugging them, and help them to abolish the road blocks,' and also 'to inject a value added and "can do" culture into the function.'

Hank Bowen – W H Smith

At W H Smith the personnel function had always been seen as a line management function. It employs specialists who are responsible for certain technical and legal aspects of personnel management, but the bottom-line responsibility belongs to directors and line managers. The vision and the initiatives on personnel management come from the chairman and the chief executive working closely with the board director responsible for personnel (staff matters) and other members of the board. There is no question of the personnel department being in a peripheral situation when business or personnel strategies and policies are formulated. As an integral part of the top management team – a line manager amongst line managers – the head of personnel contributes on an equal footing with his peers.

Rhiannon Chapman – The International Stock Exchange

Rhiannon Chapman believes that the contribution of a personnel director is as follows:

> The ability to take a dispassionate and objective view based upon credibility and an understanding of the process.

This arises because:

> The personnel director is most strongly positioned as a general-ist on the board because personnel is all-encompassing. Any question you ask is relevant to your activity whereas a specialist in a narrow range of activity doesn't have anything like the same foundation to work upon. And it's also a fabulous knowledge base because you do know, or certainly should know, more about what is going on than just about anyone else on the board. You know the people, you know the jobs they do, you know the pressures and constraints bearing on the activities they are engaged in.

The personnel director is clearly better placed than anyone else in the organization to advise on how effectively it is using its human resources. As personnel director, Rhiannon Chapman is able to:

> Identify within the organization senior people who actually have skills that we're not fully deploying and recognize that the

time has come for them to be given some other form of remit. I
can then look for opportunities to bring to the attention of the
board, the chief executive, or any of the directors individually,
the existence of these people. They may not know them or if they
do know tham their experience will be fairly narrow, whereas I
have had a wider experience of them because I've known them
longer and I've known them in different contexts.

Rhiannon Chapman thinks that:

> To be effective, the personnel function has to be led in a particu-
> lar way, and that usually boils down to the personnel director
> being someone who has a high level of personal credibility and
> professional authority. If you don't have personal credibility at
> board level you can have all the professional authority in the
> world and it won't get you anywhere. So a strong element of
> personal charisma and personal leadership has to be there.

But operating at the comparatively rarefied level of the board can result in
problems.

> The personnel director is in great danger of leaving all his or her
> people a long way behind because they are doing all the person-
> nel administration – the nitty-gritty stuff. If the personnel
> director is lucky, their respect can be gained, especially if an
> environment has been created in which they can 'do their thing'
> effectively. But it can be difficult for them to understand what
> you are there to do and how you do what you do. There really is
> an enormous gap, and actually filling that gap is the problem –
> making sure that you and your people are close enough to create
> a helpful interface.

But overriding everything else, in Rhiannon Chapman's view, is the need to
have a strong personal ethic:

> I do have a very strong personal ethic. Without it I would not
> have gone very far. And it's probably the most compelling single
> contribution that I make to the business. The reason why my
> colleagues feel any confidence in me is that they know the
> personal ethic is there, and that I won't sell individuals down the
> river and that I will take the best possible balanced view of where
> the interests of both the organization and the individual lie.

Rhiannon Chapman's objectives as Personnel Director of the International
Stock Exchange are as follows:

1 As director of the personnel and training function, to:

    (a)   assist the International Stock Exchange and the Securities
           Association to achieve its mission and objectives by pro-

viding personnel and training policies and practices which enable it to attract, retain, motivate and develop a top-quality staff, capable of achieving and delivering across a wide diversity of activities;

(b) direct and manage the personnel and training function by translating policy lines into operational activities and co-ordinating their implementation across the four operating departments, through the members of the human resources management group (HRMG);

(c) establish, motivate and lead the function in a way which allows each member of the team to develop his or her skills and deploy them to the greatest possible effect, both for individual career satisfaction and to the optimization of the resources of the team overall;

(d) develop an open, supportive and energizing relationship with the HRMG members and other senior members of the function which will ensure growing confidence in each other's activities, built on professional teamwork and personal loyalty and commitment to each other's objectives.

2 As a director of the International Stock Exchange, to contribute to business strategy and participate in business planning and the general management of the enterprise in a constructive and energizing way.

3 As personnel advisor to the chief executive and the senior management of the International Stock Exchange and the Securities Association, to contribute expertise in the area of organization and job design and to promote the effective deployment of the senior management team, through knowledge and experience of working with the senior staff and an awareness of senior staff resources in relation to resourcing needs.

4 Establish the International Stock Exchange as a leading employer in the City and, by contributing to the national employment forums, to create confidence that the International Stock Exchange and the City have the competence to manage complex employment issues with authority and to good effect.

John Crosby – BAT Industries

John Crosby refers to resourcing as a key responsibility of the personnel director.

Once a year a very detailed report is compiled which pulls together the top slice of the firm's overall succession planning process. That's a key personnel role in the centre because it's not about simply responding to events. Throughout the year one talks to the operating groups about their people, asking questions about whether there are enough people of the right quality coming through at the right time. You have to look at the quality of selection, the identification of potential, the quality of retention and the quality of training plans, as well as the relationship of these activities to business development plans.

Barry Curnow – The MSL Group

Barry Curnow believes that the contribution of personnel directors will be maximized:

> . . . by ensuring that their own viewpoint, career development and experience are firmly grounded in the business. But they must also start from the top and play their part in ensuring the teamworking, the spirit and the chemistry set a climate and tone that provides leadership by example. Some people think leadership is an old-fashioned word and associate it with the army and that sort of thing. But people want business leadership. They want management teams who stand up to be counted, who take risks and are seen to go out and be assertive and ambitious in marketplaces in order to obtain positions of leadership that will enable companies to grow.

Barry Curnow also believes that the personnel director must be committed to:

> . . . business growth and personal growth because they go hand in hand. If you want to recruit and keep good people then you have to grow the business. Businesses can't stand still. It's only through growing businesses that you can provide interesting and exciting careers. Good people will only stay and be productive and give of their best in growing, vibrant, experimental companies that take risks. And it's reciprocal. The company grows if the people grow, but the people grow and stay because the company is growing. So they're all bound up together.

Alan Fell – The Heron Corporation

In discussing his priorities, Alan Fell suggested that they could be divided into three areas. First, a whole range of personnel activities such as recruiting MDs or subsidiary company directors, restructuring the pensions fund and ensuring that psychometrics are used properly and not abused. Secondly, the involvement in corporate affairs mentioned above. Thirdly, he is concerned with 'the forward projection of the organization, in other words, where does the organization want to be down the road.'

Referring in general terms to the role of the personnel director (and using the model developed by Shaun Tyson and himself described in Chapter 2), Alan Fell thought that:

> There are some very powerful personnel directors who are in the clerk-of-works model. They'll do well for themselves and they'll retire very comfortably, and everyone will be happy, and I'm not decrying it for one minute. There are fewer major personnel directors who are operating in the contract manager role, because that role is predicated on unionization, which is not such a force nowadays. There are more personnel directors around now who are not personnel managers *manqué* but are taking up the architect model.

Peter Hobbs – Wellcome Foundation

Peter Hobbs believes that personnel directors can be very influential 'because there ought not to be anything significant happening in the organization which they don't know about.' This involves taking the initiative and saying in effect:

> 'Look, we have done this, but does that mean that there are other things involved?' And then they take people through it. I think what the personnel director should do – but it's also very dangerous – is this business of being the consultant of the organization. Someone who can actually sail in and challenge the feedback, simply saying 'Hey look, you've got to change.' In OD terms (awful phrase I know, because it can get you into too much pseudo, behavioural science nonsense, but still useful), it is the totality of the business we can look at.

In carrying out their roles personnel directors can:

> Use instruments such as training and development to get people to do things differently from the way in which they have done them before. But we must not get over-involved in techniques embodied in programmes. We ought by now to have learnt the follies of the MBO type programme which was going to be the answer to everything. There is a whole raft of consultants who have made their million simply by implying that if their nostrums were adopted just about everything was going to be fine and dandy thereafter. But the whole business of management is a great complex of different tasks held together by teamwork. And at one level personnel directors are the people who keep it running – ensuring, as it were, that the planned maintenance is done. But at another level, they are the people who say 'We have to have a totally different piece of machinery, haven't we?'

Peter Reay – Cadbury Schweppes

Peter Reay emphasizes the business-orientated role of the personnel director as follows:

> When you get to the board of management level, the Cadbury Schweppes plc board level, in a sense what you are doing is sharing in the total strategy of the business and you have just as much commitment to the achievement of the long-range targets and the annual budget as all your colleagues. On the board we largely forget our functions. We talk about the big issues that confront us: what business we should be in, what shape the business should be, what value systems, whether we should go into particular alliances in different parts of the world, the interface with the investment community and so on. We are a very small team of executive directors on the board and we do go into some detail on the big investment and marketing decisions, and I am expected to know about all these things just as my colleagues are.
>
> The personnel director, however, also has a distinctive, if you like, technical contribution to make in the fields of recruitment, training, development, organizational structure, incentives, communications and changing the culture in order to achieve much more demanding business objectives.

Lynn Richards – Halfords

Lynn Richards gave a case history of an organization going through dramatic change, moving rapidly away from an era in which people used to say 'We don't do anything like that because we've always done it like this.'

> My job as head of personnel was originally created in 1973, so that someone could come in with a background in industrial relations. Initially it wasn't seen as a personnel job in the usual sense. We had to go through a period of, if you like, ground clearing when we had to establish a proper business-like relationship with the unions rather than 'I'm going to stop the wheels and hurt you, what are you going to give me?' sort of basis, which it had been until I joined. It took until 1977 to be able to shake out the situation. It took a 10-week strike; the building was occupied. It was all highly dramatic. . . . So the job in the 1970s was to get the industrial relations situation right, otherwise we couldn't have done anything with the organization because it was being run by the full-time union official.
>
> The saving grace then, as far as we were concerned, was when we were moved from our parent company's industrial division, which had no interest in retail, to the retail distribution division.

This had a great advantage for the development of our business because the head of the division came along and asked pertinent questions, such as what market were we aiming for? What stock range? How were we representing ourselves? And he talked to me a lot about the way we were going and the need for quality people.

Fortunately, at the same time a number of the old guard were retiring, so that it was possible to change the nature of the board completely. We had the unrivalled opportunity of a new guy coming in setting new standards for the business and an almost entirely new team at the top. This is critical as far as the contribution of personnel is concerned in this business because I was responsible for selecting people who are now my colleagues, one of whom is now my boss. That's a unique position and one has always to recognize the particular context in which one is working. One can't expound universal truths about personnel.

It was in this context that it was possible to look at the controls it was necessary to exercise over the business and get answers to questions like: Have we got the right staffing structures? What's the cost basis of the business like? What is the administration like? Should we have a different structure in the branches? It all went along with a complete look at the ranges we were dealing with, the buying terms, the margin structures and the way we presented ourselves in our shops.

It is in this atmosphere that a personnel director can come into his own. I was able, first, to exert influence on the kind of organizational structure that would best fit the needs of the business as it moved through its various stages of improvement and, secondly, advise on the quality of people we wanted and the nature and style of organization needed to achieve the best possible solution without the hidebound methods that were previously used – the memoranda exchanges and all the rest of it.

The influence that an involved and entrepreneurial personnel director can have on the business was then described by Lynn Richards in the following example.

We have been very successful in recent years in developing a service orientation, but discussions with the managing director established that a big problem was left unresolved. We still got a lot of customer complaints and we didn't deal with them very well, so what could we do about that? I then started to interrogate, because our style managerially is not to look at isolated problems but to get to the fundamentals of the thing. We're always restless to improve what we're doing. That happens to be the way we work. Nobody ever takes for granted the success we're achieving. So while a superstore on the edge of town is turning over satisfactorily, it seems, at £1.5m., the question we are asking is, given that the potential of that business is £4m., what do we have to do to get there? It's that kind of process that I'm involved in as much as any of my colleagues.

So I went into the question of complaints. But when I started to probe I soon established that there was much more to it than simply dealing with customer complaints. We had to look at the whole concept of service.

The object of our exercise is to get the best product in a convenient location and sell it by providing a good sales service. But what about service after sales? The question hadn't been properly addressed. We had a cycle maintenance department and we had a customer relations department which consisted of poor harried people receiving the angry telephone calls and dealing with the irate letters. That wasn't the way to provide service.

I concluded that we had to have a function which is called service after sales, and it had to be run by a separate director, not the buying director, whose main thrust is competitiveness, margin, range development and profitability. So I brought together a proposition that said we needed service after sales and we needed to bring various related functions together under a commercial services director. He has now been appointed from within to pursue this separate specialism quite independently of his colleagues.

That's a good example of the kind of personnel involvement where you look at the organization, look at ways that it's working or not working, and then propose an alternative that will achieve a better solution. It's a kind of internal consultancy, but it isn't separate, because everything I do has to have a bottom-line impact and I'm involved all the time in discussions about the business and how we will better achieve what we need to achieve.

But I am mainly involved as a kind of balancer of teams, as someone who will look at organizations and wonder how best to structure particular responsibilities. I can then work up proposals from that and infiltrate the field, without coming forward and producing a kind of great blueprint.

Jeff Roberts – Rumbelows

My contribution is to input into the overall discussion about what we think we should achieve and are able to achieve in business terms over the next five years. I see my role as not only contributing ideas about where we should go in the medium term, but also playing devil's advocate by asking questions such as: Are these plans realistic? Can we actually achieve them? If this is what we see ourselves doing, how can we do it? What are the organizational, the people implications?

Tony Vineall – Unilever

People who hold this [a personnel director's] responsibility need to be very well informed and have within themselves a complete understanding of the overall human resource problem. These are people who would not define their basic objectives in personnel terms at all. They can be conscious in an almost painful way of how the human resource situation can be a major constraint or alternatively a major liberating factor in what they are trying to do.

How do you evaluate the contribution of the personnel directors? It's really a judgement, although there are some indicators towards that judgement. There are certain things that personnel directors would find it difficult to laugh off. They would find it hard to laugh off a very high rate of labour turnover unless there was some powerful external *force majeure*. They would find it difficult to laugh off an inability to fill jobs either by internal promotion or by external recruitment. They would find it difficult to laugh off paying the highest rates in town without some obvious benefit from doing so.

How do you lock them into the whole process of achievement? What's needed is to ensure that the human resource planning cycle mirrors the business planning cycle. This will provide the indicators which can be used for evaluation purposes. Thus the human resource review is linked to the financial and physical review systems so that targets from one relate to the targets from the other.

Peter Wickens – Nissan

I think the person, apart from the chief executive, who is best equipped to look at that strategy [for managing the business] is the personnel director. If personnel directors are not looking strategically at the way in which their company is managed, then they are not really doing the job they should be doing. So often personnel people are concerned with today's problems, today's grievances and maybe look ahead to the next negotiation, but no further. Anybody can do that. It's the easy part of the job. What really matters is totally establishing the culture of the company.

Don Young – Thorn EMI

I think the key role of personnel directors is to change the agenda of the top management group. They can influence top managers to look at the world from a different point of view, because they are or should be in a position to be predictive about the levels of performance required in all areas of the business. And if their predictions work out they will be listened to.

At this level personnel directors should not be over-concerned with the basic technologies of personnel management. Their main concern should be with the capacity of the organization to perform effectively, deliver against its mission and deal with its problems. They are there to define and establish relationships between business requirements and organizational and human requirements. They have to build a process which has coherence in the sense of what the organization should be doing over a period of time. Amongst other things this means building management strength in depth.

The skills required to do this job include: a widespread experience of management leading to a deep understanding of the fabric of the business, a profound appreciation of the factors affecting human behaviour in an organization, and well-developed counselling skills. Personnel directors do not necessarily need to be well equipped with technical skills.

CONCLUSIONS

The amount of common ground in these views about the role of the personnel director is very noticeable. The salient points emerging from them are that the personnel director is, or should be, someone who is:

- very much part of the top management team;
- involved in business planning and the integration of human resource plans with business plans;
- well placed to exert influence on the way in which the business is organized, managed and staffed – all with a view to helping it achieve its strategic objectives;
- dependent more on business awareness and skills and credibility to be effective than on professional competence in personnel techniques;
- involved heavily in resourcing at top and senior levels and in so doing is in a strong position to improve organizational effectiveness and, therefore, bottom-line performance;
- concerned with the management of change and with shaping corporate culture and values;

- fully aware of the needs to develop a vision of what the personnel function exists to do, to define its mission, to provide leadership and guidance to the members of the function (without getting involved in day-to-day personnel matters) and to maintain the quality of the support the function provides to line managers;

- essentially an enabler but one who is well placed to make a significant contribution to end results.

6 The Entrepreneurial Personnel Manager

The entrepreneurial personnel director is a recognizable and growing phenomenon. The mere fact that a personnel director is on the board indicates that some importance is attached to the function. And even if some appointments to the board have been token ones, and many personnel directors have only got there because they are good at industrial relations fire-fighting, the fact remains that once there, they are given the opportunity to get really involved in the business.

This seems to be more difficult to achieve at levels below the personnel director, or where the personnel manager is not on the board and reports to someone with a mysterious title like administration director. In these circumstances personnel managers may not participate directly in strategic issues. If they report to a personnel director who does get them involved then they will have the opportunity to take an entrepreneurial line, which means ensuring that the advice and support services provided are aimed specifically at achieving benefits which will further the company's objectives. If they are not fortunate enough to be placed in that position, they may have to struggle a bit. But 'say not the struggle nought availeth, the end is not the goal.' In other words, even if personnel managers are not directly in a position to achieve ends they can, if they try hard enough, get themselves in positions where they can through various forms of intervention exact considerable influence on the means towards those ends.

THE NEED TO INTERVENE

There is a whole raft of things that personnel managrs have to do and administer. They recruit, they train, they run the salary system, they ensure that the legal and social obligations of the company are met, they deal with day-to-day employee relations issues and grievances, and they maintain a personnel database. If they do these things efficiently they will make a contribution to the bottom line, although it may seem remote and it will be difficult to measure. Their activities must be seen to be cost-effective, but to what extent are they or can they be profit-effective?

70

There is always a danger in personnel management, if it is perceived mainly as an administrative function, of spending too much time making ineffective organizations efficient. And that never works. Progress, development, growth, added value are achieved by positive drives to improve all-round effectiveness rather than by negative cost or paper reduction exercises.

Mike Stanton sees personnel managers as facilitators but also as questioners who are looking at wider issues.

> Even if the human resource function understands the business and does a good job at board level of building the human resource aspects into business strategy, the implementation and delivery of the people strategy has to rest in the hands of line managers and not directly in the personnel function. Personnel managers very often have to be facilitators and catalysts. They can do the basic research on where the human resource aspects of the busines are so that they can hold that up and say 'Look where we are now, and it's not looking like where we want to be, so what are we going to do about bridging the gap?'
>
> I don't think we are always as successful as we might be as personnel people in getting across to line managers where the dividing line is between the human resource specialist needling, posing questions and formulating strategies and the line manager doing things and delivering. A lot of companies still misunderstand that divide and say 'Well, you know, we want to contract, or we want to expand, or we want people to be better motivated, and that's the responsibility of the personnel manager.' But it isn't. It's the responsibility of the personnel function to provide the environment in which line management can achieve these things but it's not within the power of the function to deliver it.

But as facilitators, catalysts, enablers, change agents and creators of environments conducive to successful accomplishment, personnel managers have to intervene. They cannot contribute from a supine position.

Tony Vineall sees personnel managers as being concerned with the implementation and monitoring of policies but also with 'selective intervention': 'You need to dive in and get really involved.'

> As well as defining policies you need to monitor what's going on with as little paperwork as you can. You must try very hard to keep down the bureaucracy. On the basis of that, you intervene selectively. First you find methods of monitoring what's happening in a simple way, then you act.
>
> You intervene in different ways in different situations, and it's an opportunistic business. You have to start with an overview of where the pressure points are in an organization and where you

can make a useful intervention. But the opportunity to intervene can come at the most unexpected times.

For instance, if you are getting frustrated over filling a job and two or three top-line executives are equally frustrated, you have a window there through which you can harness that frustration to achieve longer-term aims. And doing it opportunistically can be much more effective than writing a long report at a time when they're not interested in the problem.

One doesn't always work like that but it can often be a highly personalized job. If you have this responsibility and take this line you need to be well informed and have inside yourself an understanding of the overall human resources problem. And with this understanding you can deal with people who would not define their basic objectives in personnel terms at all. You can take advantage of the moments when they are, almost in a painful way, conscious of how the human resource situation is a major constraint or, alternatively, a major liberating factor of what they're trying to do. So one has to be opportunistic. But don't overdo it.

How else do you make interventions? In some complicated circumstances it is very helpful to have the mechanism of an annual review of the human resource situation. The skill of the human resource specialist is first of all to spot the problem. You can just look at some facts which would perhaps get nodded through by people who aren't used to them and spot the structure of the situation. You can see what's going wrong. It's a skill and it's a skill acquired over time.

You can get insights into general problems through particular problems. You can't make the progress you want and then you realize that there's a bigger and more general problem building up. I think that an understanding of underlying personnel problems comes to you by looking at actual situations and solving actual problems rather than going through some process of analysis which starts with all the facts.

Now we've agreed that the personnel manager is an enabler, so how do we reconcile the intervener with the enabler? Let's take the example of recruitment. Personnel managers don't make appointments. There is no organization in the world where the personnel manager makes appointments. Therefore in the end they have to convince, to influence, people who are making the appointment to make a decision in the interests of the whole organization. This would be the sort of decision they would not take if they had a narrow view of what would make their life better over the next three years. You're never going to be in a situation where you can overrule the individual although you can come close to doing so by ensuring that the issue gets considered at a higher level.

SEIZING THE DAY

Personnel managers contribute to the bottom line by providing efficient administrative services. They select and use appropriate technology. They may feel – rightly or wrongly – that they are in the business of social engineering, helping to build and maintain the machinery of organization, which is a social mechanism involving the actions and interactions of people. If they do this they should remember Karl Popper's words in *The poverty of historicism*:

> Social engineering resembles physical engineering in regarding the *ends* as beyond the province of technology.

Personnel techniques are means towards the achievement of ends. Personnel managers may have to accept these ends as given. They have to concentrate on developing and implementing personnel technologies which are relevant to the ends and will contribute to their achievement, but they are not ends in themselves. These ends, the superordinate goals of the organization, exist in their own right. Of course personnel managers can and should attempt to influence them, but this is not achieved by introducing techniques as panaceas or nostrums. Many years ago in *The practice of management*, Peter Drucker posed the question 'Is personnel bankrupt?' His answer was that it wasn't, but it would be if personnel managers felt that they had to use techniques and gimmicks as props to support their professional prestige.

Good personnel managers make an impact on the achievements of their organization by using their personal perceptions and skills to influence the recruitment, retention, utilization, organization, motivation and development of people. The end is improved performance and that is why they are as much performance managers as personnel managers. The means are interventions as described by Tony Vineall. These are prompted by an appreciation of where the organization is going and an understanding of the processes that will get it there and of the pressure points that might get in the way. As Tony Vineall said, personnel managers have to be opportunistic. They have to seize the day and grab whatever opportunities present themselves to exert influence for the good of the organization and its members.

Such opportunities are happening all the time. Personnel managers should never feel that they are unable to exert influence, even if they are operating at a tactical rather than a strategic level. Organizations can print and distribute as many mission statements as they like but they are meaningless if they do not prompt appropriate action. And they will be much more meaningful if they are prompted by action and practice, by the processes of people management that go on at the grass roots. These are the processes with which personnel managers and officers are involved, whether they are covering all the personnel functions at plant level or whether they are specialists in training, remuneration, recruitment, industrial relations or any other area of human resource management.

It is remarkable how much can be done by being opportunistic at the tactical or grass-roots level. Gordon Sapsed of IBM comments that, from his own experience, 40 per cent of the personnel manager's time is spent in dealing with problems that arise and are solved in the same day. But these problems, if analyzed and assessed properly, can provide plenty of clues on how to spend the remaining 60 per cent more positively.

Peter Hobbs starts from the point that there ought not to be anything going on concerning the management of people in the organization that the personnel manager does not know about. That gives personnel managers the power to influence things at the bottom end. He quotes an example from his early career in a large organization when he came across a statistical return about works council arrangements and said 'What's this for?' When no one could give a coherent answer he said 'Let's abolish it'. It was not for another eight or more years that he found out that abolishing this return had effectively changed the consultative structure of the firm. 'And it wasn't until I was at a much more senior level and suddenly put two and two together that I realized that as a tiny cog in the machine I had actually changed the direction of the thing.'

> So this is the great lesson. If you know the stuff at the bottom, and do the right things down there, it can be much more effective in terms of the impact it will make than in getting the lord high boss to say 'I endorse this,' writing slogans or whatever else.

Don Young quotes another example of his experience as a training officer at Birds Eye Foods. he was presented with what line management perceived as a training problem. This was concerned with the yield from filleting fish – getting down to the bare bones of the matter, as it were! It was felt that if the fish filleters were given extra training, a contribution to the bottom line of half a million or so could be achieved. Don Young quickly saw that this was not just a training problem, if it were one at all. It was instead a mix of problems concerning work methods, layouts, organization, skills and an overall lack of understanding of what yields could be achieved and how to get them. So he was instrumental in setting up an inter-disciplinary project team which looked at all aspects of the problem and came up with solutions which significantly increased yield and performance.

The writer, as a unit personnel manager in what was then the British Aircraft Corporation (now British Aerospace), was presented with a problem which was turned into an opportunity. It concerned the retention of skilled craftsmen who were responsible for final assembly. They were being recruited at considerable expense from all over the kingdom but were lasting for no more than a few weeks. The success of the project depended on getting *and* keeping them. It was a retention not a recruitment problem. Comparative analysis showed that there was no difficulty in keeping people in the fitting shops where the units for final assembly were manufactured – so, why the difference?

The answer was almost distressingly obvious and simple. Everyone was on an individual time-saved bonus scheme. There was no work measurement. Times were set by people who were aptly known as rate fixers, and as far as they and everyone else of the shop floor were concerned, 'fixing' was the name of the game. A continuous process of haggling took place between rate fixers, shop stewards and fitters over the rate for the job. In the fitting shops this did not present a special problem. The work flowed continuously, modifications were few and far between, the rates were well established and earnings were steady and predictable. In the assembly halls life was quite different. Modifications abounded, work came in fits and starts, parts were not available at the kit marshalling store, rates were not fixed, so that haggling was the order of the day and, consequently, earnings fluctuated and were quite unpredictable.

Diagnosis means working back from symptoms to causes. Causality in this case consisted of a complex web of inter-relating factors. Assemblers did not stay long with the company because, living away from home as most of them did, they had to be able to predict their earnings. Because of the bonus scheme they were unable to do so, and the scheme was not working because of the modifications, the intermittent flow of work, the unavailability of parts and so on.

There was no simple answer. A task force was set up on the recommendation of the personnel department led by the production manager and with representatives from production engineering, the design and development departments and personnel. It successfully reduced the negative impact of the flow of modifications and design changes, it reorganized the kit marshalling store, it introduced a 'stage build' system consisting of work teams with clearly defined targets for each stage and with some scope for self-regulation, and it introduced procedures for smoothing out fluctuations. It also had a go at the bonus scheme itself, but this was too deeply entrenched, and a longer-term project was set up to look into the scheme in depth.

The result of the task force's efforts was a significant reduction in labour wastage but, more importantly, it brought different and often warring factions together to fight a common cause, and produced some fundamental new thinking about methods of working and of managing people. In this case, the personnel manager acted as the catalyst. Without his intervention it is unlikely that the inter-disciplinary approach which was evolved could have got off the ground.

HOW TO BE AN ENTREPRENEURIAL PERSONNEL MANAGER

There are five things personnel managers need to do to be more entrepreneurial.

1 Be business-like

Entrepreneurial personnel managers are business people first. Alan Fell remarked in this connection that if he were recruiting a personnel manager for an entrepreneurial and growing business he would favour applicants with line management as well as personnel experience. He would look for the sort of person who, when shown a set of accounts:

> . . . will be able to read it and say 'I see what you mean, we've got to do something about *that*', pointing to it.

Peter Hobbs suggests that:

> . . . there is very much a role for the personnel manager here, but it does require special skills. I don't think people can do it unless they have actually been through some form of apprenticeship lower down to acquire a knowledge of the nuts and bolts. So then they know what you actually can and cannot do further up.

2 Get involved

Personnel managers must get involved in the business and with the people who run the business. They must know what is going on. Perhaps the most practical of all personnel techniques is PMBWA: personnel management by walking about. Thus they can find out what people as well as the business need and want. Using their antennae they can spot symptoms and, using their diagnostic skills (an important attribute), they can identify causes and solutions to the problems. If they want to get anything done they know that managers must 'own' both the problem and its solution. Close involvement means that personnel people can become adept at transferring ownership.

Terry Murphy commented on the problems which arise when the personnel function is not 'interweaved with the fabric of the operation'. He referred to some personnel managers who, when their company is developing a new product, never think of the training needs that this generates, and others who would not be able to contemplate the human resource needs created by a new business development.

3 Intervene effectively

Personnel managers have to use this knowledge and awareness of business needs to select the right place and time to intervene. It can be difficult. Peter Hobbs refers to an actual case (not in his present firm) where:

> . . . people suddenly found a whole series of new techniques and opportunities opened up to them, but were unable to impact on the organization. They could see these great golden opportunities to do much better but they couldn't persuade anyone. They couldn't get access, they couldn't do anything, and they 'died of broken hearts'.

4 Be persuasive

Intervention of the kind described earlier in this chapter can open doors and get things done, especially if the personnel manager is persuasive. Tom Davis, Managing Director of Hewlett-Packard's sales and marketing division in the UK, emphasized the need for personnel managers to take 'a broad overall view of the business'.[1] They need to know about the 'correlation between business success and progressive personnel policies'. And, above all, they have to persuade:

> Personnel managers who do not recognize that they are in the persuasion business are doomed to carry on being seen in the traditional bureaucratic image.

According to Tom Davis, personnel managers are too often the 'harbingers of doom', telling everyone what will go wrong if they don't follow their advice and in effect training their managements to think of them as talking only of disasters. The answer to this problem is that personnel people must persuade management to invest in systems where they have demonstrated that there is a pay-off. As Tom Davis says:

> Instead of being the 'harbingers of doom', personnel can become the innovators of excellence and the accelerators of productivity.

5 Be a realist

Being a realist means recognizing the law of the situation, the logic of facts and events. It means that:

(a) ideas for improvement or innovation are thoroughly tested against an analysis of the characteristics and the true needs of the organization;

(b) proposals are sold to management on the basis of the practical and, wherever possible, measurable benefits that will result from their implementation – it is not the idea itself that is saleable but the worthwhile result it can achieve;

(c) recommendations on policy or on the adoption of new procedures or techniques are presented to management as providing direct help to them in running the business or their department more effectively than before;

(d) the support services provided are not just cost-effective, they are also profit-effective in that the people recruited, the training they are given, the reward system provided for them, the appraisal procedures used and the working environment that has been created are all contributing to improved organizational performance in measurable ways.

What entrepreneurial personnel managers cannot be is purists. This is how Alan Fell put it:

> If you put in a purist who had only ever operated from one perspective, I know that in any organization, which is about making new money, not just re-allocating it, he would probably not survive. He would not be credible to line managers. He would not be co-equal if he kept on saying 'You can't do that' and 'No, it's not the practice of my Institution', or 'No, when I last went to Harrogate they told me not to do it that way.'

PERSONAL QUALITIES

To be effective in the current economic, social and political climate personnel managers must be entrepreneurial. They will not, however, be good entrepreneurs unless they possess certain personal qualities. In Tony Vineall's view:

> First of all they need all the basic things that businessmen need. They need to understand figures, they need to be articulate, they need to be able to convince others, and so on. I think they have to satisfy many of the requirements of the business world but they have to derive satisfaction from leading from behind. There are few victories for the personnel function that go up in coloured lights. Victories of that sort are concerned with the introduction of the new management by objectives scheme, or something like that. And I don't regard these as real victories.

Reference

1   Davis, Tom. 'How personnel can lose its Cinderella image'. *Personnel Management*. December 1987, pp 34–36

7 The Impact of the Personnel Function on the Bottom Line

IS IT POSSIBLE?

The answer to this question is simple and blindingly obvious. People are the ultimate source of value. Personnel management activities have a major impact on individual performance and therefore must also impact on productivity and organizational performance. They do this by taking a strategic and integrated view of human resource management, by helping to shape the culture and values of the organization and by ensuring that these promote commitment and the successful pursuit of quality and excellence.

Peter Reay referred to the Cadbury Schweppes approach as follows:

> The culture of this business has been significantly changed and the personnel function has helped to achieve that. The big lesson for me, and it's not in the least original, is that what you have to do is to make sure that the total system is integrated and internally consistent. There's no point in hiring aggressive entrepreneurial people and then having a reward system which disqualifies them from benefiting from their talents and which penalizes them every time they take a risk and make a mistake. There is no point at all in having a terrific vision of the future at the top of the business if what is being communicated down through the hierarchy is actually something which is extremely boring and inconsistent with the vision. There's absolutely no point in preaching a different level of performance and then carrying on running routine training programmes which don't reflect the change in style and standards that you are trying to achieve.
>
> It seems to me that what you've got to do – what we've tried to do – is to make sure that we move ahead on all fronts: structure, the basic competence of our workforce, the recruitment and training which that requires, the investment in development, communication and, extremely importantly, reward. All these things have got to hang together.

So if you ask me what the personnel function can do to promote profitability, my answer is that it must make sure that all the services it renders, all the skills it provides, all the specialist insights it is paid to deliver, together support the total commercial objective of the business and all reinforce one another.

An impact on the bottom line is possible if you take the integrated view as advocated by Peter Reay and adopt Lynn Richards' approach:

Look at the organization. Look at the ways in which it is working or not working and propose alternatives that will achieve a better solution. Everything I do has to have a bottom-line impact and I'm involved all the time in the business and how we can better achieve what we need to achieve.

IS IT DESIRABLE?

Some personnel people think that they are into social engineering, almost as an end in itself. They are concerned with the technology of the process and would happily accept Sir Karl Popper's belief that the ends are beyond the province of technology. With them, it is not a question of the ends justifying the means. It is more a case of the means justifying themselves, for their own sakes.

Perhaps this is a hangover from the 1960s' 'flower people' approach of the more extreme behavioural scientists with their belief in the virtues of trust, love, openness and sharing, and 'a new concept of organization values, based on humanistic-democratic ideals'.[1] This, however, was accompanied by their failure to recognize the existence of commercial and technological constraints. Their ideological and worthy concern for personal development and the rights of the individual did not take account of the realities of organizational life such as competitiveness, ambition, power plays, distrust and dislike, and the fact that organizations exist to deliver results.

There are, of course, dangers in the unswerving pursuit of profitability. This can be at the expense of the individual members of the organization. Only asset strippers benefit from asset stripping. The values of the behavioural scientists are worthwhile and should be part of the value set of any organization. Organizations do have responsibilities to all their stakeholders, and these certainly include their employees. They must be concerned with providing scope to use and develop natural talents, with being even-handed, and with providing equal opportunities, security of employment, a high quality of working life and a healthy and safe working environment.

But personnel people must be realistic and appreciate that these highly desirable goals can only be achieved if the organization prospers, and it is their job to help the organization to prosper. They do not have to accept the undesirable values and behaviours that exist in organizations, but in striving to correct these they have still to direct their overall efforts into the

improvement of organizational performance to the benefit of all concerned.
They have to be prepared to go along with the sentiments expressed in the
Eldridge Pope 1985 Director's Report as quoted by Peter Wickens:

> We invest large amounts of time and money in involving
> employees in the operation and success of the business, and our
> objective is quite simply increasing success as measured by
> growing profits. It is profits which sustain the present and equip
> the future, giving property and security to the whole team,
> shareholders and employees alike.[2]

HOW IS IT DONE?

If it is accepted that a business orientation towards the bottom-line performance on the part of personnel managers is both possible and desirable,
then the next question to be answered is how can it be done? The starting
point to answering that question is an appreciation of the factors in organizations that contribute to better bottom-line results. Against this background general approaches can be developed which aim to enhance added
value and increase competitive advantage. At the same time a continuous
review of the objectives and activities of the personnel function is carried
out to ensure that these are integrated with and support the achievement of
business objectives.

Factors affecting bottom-line performance

There is no universally applicable list of factors that affect bottom-line
performance. Each organization is unique.

But there are a number of common elements. The orientations listed
below certainly exist in Book Club Associates, a highly successful company.
And in one form or other they exist in the leading British based companies
contacted in researching for this book. Successful businesses, measured in
bottom-line or any other terms, are likely to be:

1 *Market orientated*   They:
- are good at identifying and exploiting market opportunities;
- know that the organization exists and thrives by delivering value to its customers;
- are therefore fully aware of the need to relate to and care for their customers;
- seek competitive advantage in all they do.

2 *Business orientated*   They:
- know what business they are in;

- know what they are good at;
- 'stick to their knitting'[3] – they stay close to the business they know and make the best use of the knowledge, expertise and resources that have created success.

3 *Growth orientated* They:

- go for growth;
- build market share;
- constantly strive to achieve real improvement based on competitive gain.

4 *Innovation orientated* They:

- know that their business must be capable of continuous renewal;
- appreciate that innovation evokes demand and creates market momentum;
- develop strategies which are agendas for change and aim to convert visions into reality;
- give members of the organization 'the freedom and power to consummate their entrepreneurial ideas';[4]
- develop organizations which promote flexibility and the capacity to respond rapidly to challenge and change;
- see the business as a learning organization, continually analyzing and using experience in order to stimulate and manage change.

5 *Action orientated* They:

- seize opportunities;
- make things happen – fast;
- emphasize performance and results, not process;
- give people 'the freedom to act which arouses the desire to act'.[5]

6 *Profit orientated* They:

- see every opportunity as a profit opportunity;
- press relentlessly for revenue enhancement and higher added value;
- pursue cost-effectiveness by eliminating unnecessary administrative expense but maintain their thrust towards profit-effectiveness – investing in success and achieving a higher rate of return on that investment.

7 *Quality orientated* They:

- pursue excellence in all they do;

- believe, as at Nissan, in 'quality above all';
- design and build quality into the product;
- make total quality improvement a way of life.

8 *Value orientated* By means of top management leadership and example they:

- are value driven;
- develop 'a culture of pride and a climate of success';[6]
- create a shared agenda for all who work in the organization.

9 *Team orientated* They:

- see effective teamwork as an essential ingredient for organizational success;
- promote good teamwork by:
  - using inter-disciplinary task forces;
  - encouraging involvement in formulating objectives, planning and decision-making;
  - flattening and loosening organization structures to stimulate co-operation and communication across what were formerly rigid departmental or hierarchical boundaries;
  - using the matrix organization to enforce an integrative approach;
  - deliberately allowing ambiguities and overlaps in the allocation of responsibility to discourage segmentation and make managers reach beyond the bounds of their job;
  - allocating work and setting goals for teams rather than individuals.

10 *People orientated* They:

- recognize that while orientations such as those listed above are essential for success, each of them is utterly dependent on the quality, expertise, motivation and involvement of the organization's human resources. In other words, growth, innovation, quality and performance can only be achieved by people;
- believe in the exercise of transformational leadership which, as an architect of change, shares its vision of the future with the members of the organization and enlists their total support in its achievement.

And the last shall be first. Value is created by people, who are the highest common factor in organizational achievement. That is why the personnel function can make a most significant and lasting contribution to the bottom line.

The overall approach

Barry Curnow gave the following answer to the question of how the personnel function can contribute to success:

I think this is a very good time to ask that question. We've moved through periods when money has been in short supply and when technology has been in short supply. Now it's the people who are in short supply. So we are now better placed than ever before to make a real difference, a numerical difference, a bottom-line difference, a difference that can add to shareholders' values, which at the end of the day is the most visible lasting measure although it may not be the best one.

What I see happening now is that it is those companies where importance is attached to people and to people development who have the competitive edge. As I've said, there's plenty of money around now. Some people might say far too much and more than is good for business. And there's plenty of technology. Again, many people would say far too much. So the scarce resource, which is the people resource, really is the one that makes the difference at the margin, that makes one firm competitive over another.

John Hougham at Ford sees his team as 'pushing the business forward':

In almost no sense are we into social engineering. There is very little of what we do which is some bright idea of the personnel department – 'Wouldn't it be nice if. . . .' One thing that is very true about Ford is that the bottom line is pre-eminent. We are driven, all of us, whatever function we are in, as businessmen. We are driven to think as businessmen and we are driven to look at the business relationship between what we do and the end results. And I have to account for that.

Obviously there are sometimes things we decide ought to be done because we are professionals in our own field and we are looking at whatever it might be – training, developing a new programme with the trade unions – and it might not have an obvious bottom-line effect. But I still have to account for that. I still have to persuade people that it is a profitable road to go down – profitable in the widest sense.

This overall approach is concerned with resourcing in a business environment in two areas which impact directly on the bottom line – added value and competitive advantage.

Added value
Added value is the difference between the income of the business arising from sales (output) and the amount spent on materials and other purchased services (input). Added value is partly created because the firm has capital resources, financial reserves and goodwill, which are owned by the shareholders and, in so far as they represent financial investments, must generate a return to those who made the investment. This return is taken from added value in the form of dividends or rights issues, as is any money

required to pay taxes and interest on loans, or for retention in the business.

Give the financial base, however, added value is entirely created by the employees of the company, who get their return in pay, benefits and, sometimes, profit shares or share options. It is up to these people to ensure that financial resources are invested wisely and productively and that there is an adequate pay-off from investments in technology, physical resources, research, development and marketing. It is also up to employees to make, buy and sell quality products profitably, to improve productivity, to provide good customer care, to reduce costs per unit of output and to manage the business cost-effectively.

The concept of added value can also be used more broadly to cover any increase that can be gained on the normal return that would be expected from the investment of the time and energy of people into manufacturing, providing and selling a product or service. This increase would be measured in terms of greater profitability, improved quality or better service.

A third way of looking at added value is from the customers' point of view. A product or service has added value and will successfully compete for their attention if it offers more for the price they pay than alternative products. Added value will be assessed by them in terms of better quality, better after-sales service, greater relevance to their particular needs and, of course, value for money.

In each of these three cases, the achievement of added value depends on people: managers planning, organizing, directing and exercising leadership to get improved performance from their teams, and the members of those teams responding and co-operating accordingly. Ultimately, added value is created by their efforts, endeavours and expertise. The personnel function enhances added value by ensuring that people with these motivations are available and by helping to create a culture and environment which stimulates higher levels of quality performance.

Competitive advantage
Competitive edge is achieved by innovation, marketing and providing, at a price, better quality and higher levels of customer service. It is not achieved in the long run simply by cutting costs or prices. The personnel function has the responsibility of helping top management to create an organization and an environment which is conducive to innovation, which encourages 'intrapreneurs' and is dedicated to total quality.

A successful personnel approach to increasing competitive advantage was described by Peter Wickens as helping to construct a tripod, the three legs of which are flexibility, quality consciousness and teamworking. 'Like all tripods it is indivisible and interdependent – lose one leg and the structure falls.'[7] This is the philosophy that drives Nissan, and the personnel function is very much involved in getting it put into practice.

Planning and budgeting for improved bottom-line performance

As it represents the difference between sales revenue and the costs incurred in generating those sales, bottom-line performance can obviously be improved either by increasing sales or by reducing the costs of sales and overheads. Profit improvement programmes concentrate on:

1 Increasing sales revenue
2 Improving the gross maragin (sales revenue less the cost of sales)
3 Increasing productivity
4 Reducing overheads.

This book takes a positive view of the contribution that can be made by the personnel function to the bottom line. The emphasis is on improving performance by increasing sales from existing and new products and markets. Hence the importance attached to obtaining commitment to growth, innovation, performance and quality and to motivating people to work more effectively and productively. But it is necessary also to adopt a profit approach to the planning and budgeting of all personnel activities.

Personnel planning for profit
Going for growth is the best approach, but it has to be profitable growth. So everything that the personnel department does must be governed by its profit effectiveness. This means reviewing its strategies, plans and programmes and specifying objectives in terms of their contribution to improved performance and productivity. Critical success factors should be established and, wherever possible, performance measures should be identified as a means of comparing achievements with aims in all these areas:

• *training*, where the emphasis should be on performance-related training which involves action learning and is directed towards specific and measurable improvements;

• *management development*, where a competency approach is used to identify what managers have to be able to do to be effective in their present jobs and to be promoted;

• *performance management*, where the emphasis is on measuring performance and planning ways of improving it;

• *paying for performance*, where all performance-related pay schemes are constructed to achieve improved results either by providing a direct incentive and/or by indicating the areas where priority should be given to performance improvement;

• *commitment*, gaining commitment to core values concerned with quality and customer service and creating a performance orientated culture;

• *employee relations*, devising employee relations strategies which seek to enlist the continuing support of trade unions to increasing productivity in specified ways in accordance with the principle of mutuality – shared responsibility and shared rewards.

Profit-related budgeting

The basic approach to profit-related budgeting is output budgeting. This is the concept of examining every input (expenditure), assessing the outputs that will ensue and evaluating whether an acceptable contribution to the bottom line will be achieved.

Another approach is to use the zero base budgeting technique, which would mean that the personnel department would regularly have to justify every item of expense in terms of its value to the business. In effect, this involves rebuilding the budget from scratch every year.

A more refined method is priority based budgeting which, like zero base budgeting, involves a radical reappraisal of the costs and value-for-money of activities, but also assesses priorities between different activities, helps to allocate resources to achieve strategic objectives and provides increased funding for priority areas by re-allocating the cost savings made elsewhere.

Contribution to productivity improvement

Productivity is the relationship between inputs and outputs. It can be expressed as an index by means of a series of ratios:

$$\frac{\text{productivity}}{\text{index}} = \frac{\text{output}}{\text{input}} = \frac{\text{performance achieved}}{\text{resources consumed}} = \frac{\text{effectiveness}}{\text{efficiency}}$$

Productivity is not simply performance nor the economic use of resources, but a combination of both. The emphasis in this book has been mainly on the positive steps that personnel managers can take to improve performance, but the personnel function can make a notable contribution to achieving the more economic use of resources, thus improving productivity.

The most typical productivity ratios are:

- $\dfrac{\text{units produced or processed}}{\text{number of employees}}$

- $\dfrac{\text{sales turnover}}{\text{number of employees}}$

- $\dfrac{\text{added value}}{\text{number of employees}}$

- $\dfrac{\text{net profit}}{\text{number of employees}}$

- $\dfrac{\text{standard hours produced}}{\text{number of employees}}$

The common element of these ratios is, of course, the number of employees. Productivity may be improved by the use of new technology but it is achieved mainly through the more efficient and effective use of human resources: i.e., productivity through people. The following check list highlights the areas that should be examined when planning and conducting a productivity campaign.

Productivity Check List

Planning, budgeting and control

1 Are productivity performance targets and standards defined, attainable and measurable?

2 Are individuals aware of the targets and standards they are expected to achieve?

3 Do human resource plans and budgets specifically take into account the productivity improvements that can be achieved in order to reduce human resource costs?

4 Is a zero base or priority base budgeting approach used to justify and prioritize human resource expenditures in terms of the outputs to be achieved?

5 Does this budgeting approach not only subject requests for additonal people to close scrutiny but also require budget holders to justify existing staff levels?

6 Does the approach assess priorities between different activities by reference to the contribution they will make to achieving short- and long-term objectives?

7 Do control reports identify variances from the budget?

8 Are managers and supervisors accountable for such variances?

9 Is there evidence that corrective action is being taken successfully to correct adverse variances?

Work methods

10 Is there a continuous drive to review and improve work methods in all parts of the organization?

11 Is the method improvement programme supported wholeheartedly from the top?

12 Has the programme the support of managers, supervisors, employees generally and trade unions? If not:

13 What steps are being taken to secure support?

14 Is the programme producing measurable improvements in productivity?

Work measurement

15   Is work measurement used wherever possible to develop standards, give better control information and improve methods and procedures?

16   Is work measurement used to provide the basis for effective incentive schemes?

New technology

17   In introducing new technology, is full consideration given to:
     (a) the impact it will make on productivity;
     (b) the need to train people properly in its use;
     (c) the need to gain acceptance for the new technology from employees and trade unions?

Paying for performance

18   Are paying for performance (payment by results) schemes used to boost productivity wherever appropriate?

19   Wherever possible, are the schemes based on work measurement or the achievement of quantifiable and stretching targets and standards?

20   Are effective measures taken to control 'wage drift', i.e. increases in pay not related to increases in productivity?

21   Has consideration been given to the introduction of gain-sharing schemes, i.e. bonuses for all employees related to an overall measure of performance such as added value?

22   Is there a profit sharing scheme which, even if it does not have a direct impact on output, can be used to increase commitment by demonstrating that the company is prepared to share productivity gains with its employees?

Training

23   Do analyses of training needs concentrate on the competences required to improve performance and productivity?

24   Are training programmes geared to producing measurable improvements in performance and productivity?

25   Is training followed up and evaluated to make sure that it is achieving its productivity gain objectives?

References

1   BENNIS, W. *Organizational development*. Reading. Mass. Addison Wesley, 1960
2   WICKENS, Peter. *The road to Nissan*. London. Macmillan, 1987
3   PETERS, Tom *and* WATERMAN, Robert. *In search of excellence*. New York. Harper & Row, 1982
4   GILDER, George. *The spirit of enterprise*. New York. Simon & Schuster, 1984
5   KANTER, Rosabeth Moss. *The change masters*. London. Allen & Unwin, 1984
6   *Ibid.*
7   WICKENS. *op. cit.*

8 Human Resource Strategy and the Bottom Line

THE IMPORTANCE OF STRATEGIC HUMAN RESOURCE MANAGEMENT

It is the people who implement the business plan. Strategic human resource management recognizes this fact by taking a broader, more integrated view of the personnel function, linking it firmly to the achievement of the long-term strategies of the organization and ensuring that personnel people provide the guidance and expert support needed to accomplish the strategies.

Aims of human resource strategy

The aims of human resource strategy are to enable the business to achieve its targets for growth and prosperity by:

- ensuring that all business planning processes recognize from the outset that the ultimate source of value is people;

- seeing that all concerned in strategic planning appreciate the human resource implications of their proposals and understand the potential human resource constraints if action is not taken;

- achieving a close match between corporate business objectives and the objectives of the human resource function;

- designing and managing the culture, climate and organizational processes of the business to make sure that they help everyone to do their jobs better and assist in getting and keeping high calibre people;

- Identifying the firm's distinctive competences and the types of people who will be needed to build and maintain them;

- ensuring that the resourcing activities of the business will contribute in

91

specified ways to the development of the firm's competences in the
short- and long-term;

- assessing the performance requirements needed to reach the company's
  goals and deciding the lines along which the requirements should be
  satisfied;

- reviewing the levels of commitment throughout the organization and
  planning ways to improve them where necessary.

Human resource strategy as an integral part of the business plan

Strategic human resource management is not simply an add-on to the
corporate plan. It is, or should be, an integral part of it. Business strategies
must take into account the human implications of the plans *as they are being
formulated.*

The business plan should be based on a strategic vision of where it is
believed the company should be going. Turning that vision into reality is a
matter of defining the mission of the company and then setting its goals and
developing strategic plans for their achievement.

The goals will refer to growth, by expansion from the present base and/or
acquisition, market development, product development, the introduction
of new technology and, perhaps, the preservation of the business from
external threats. Strategies will be concerned not only with plans but also
with the capability of the business to accomplish its goals. Capability will be
related to the supply of financial, technical, systems and physical resources,
but, equally importantly, it will depend on the availability of the human
resource and how that resource is made available, organized, developed
and motivated.

To make sure that full consideration is given during the strategic planning
process to human resource implications the following questions need to be
answered.

Human resource strategy checklist

1 Is the corporate culture as manifested in its core values, climate and
   management style, supportive or dysfunctional?

2 Will the structure of the organization and the way it operates be capable
   of responding appropriately to the challenges ahead?

3 What sort of people and how many of them will be required?

4 Could growth and development plans be constrained because of shortages of people with the right abilities and skills?

5 Are levels of performance throughout the organization high enough to
   meet the new demands for innovation, increased profitability, higher
   productivity and better quality?

6   Are levels of commitment to the organization and its values sufficiently high?

7   Are there any other potential constraints in achieving goals such as lack of co-operation from trade unions?

Human resource strategy areas

These questions and the answers to them will define the areas in which human resource strategies will need to be developed such as:

- *culture change* – developing a more appropriate and functional corporate culture;

- *organization planning and development* – restructuring the organization and increasing the effectiveness of organizational processes such as teamwork and communications;

- *resourcing* – providing the human resources required by recruitment, training and developing;

- *performance management* – improving the performance of individuals and therefore the organization by such means as performance appraisal, performance-related training and paying for performance;

- *commitment* – training, communication and people management programmes designed to gain and maintain commitment;

- *employee relations* – the development of policies, plans and approaches which will enhance mutuality, i.e. maximizing the degree to which management and employees will co-operate to their mutual benefit and minimizing the causes and effects of conflict or restrictive practices. This will cover such matters as recognition policy, the nature of agreements, and longer-term negotiating strategies.

The three guiding principles in developing personnel strategies are, first, that they should be linked clearly to the corporate plan; secondly, that they should support the achievement of the plan; and thirdly, that they should make specific contributions to bottom-line performance.

Before examining how personnel strategies are developed in practice, however, it is necessary to consider the context within which they are formulated. This means examining the role of strategy in an organization, what business strategies there are and how they are translated into corporate plans.

THE ROLE OF STRATEGY

The bottom line, as Peter Drucker points out, 'is indeed the ultimate test of business performance'.[1] Profit represents the outcome of numerous complex decisions. These decisions need to be integrated and co-ordinated and consistent plans of action need to be developed.

Strategy is what makes the whole add up to more than the sum of its parts. It defines the means towards ends. It is directive, channelling enterprise and energy so that they flow towards where the organization wants to go. As Peter Wickens says:

> The job must be to say: 'Today we look like this, in five years time we want to look like that. . . . It's about management having the perception of what it is possible to achieve and then having the will to make it happen. If you've got the will but not the perception then you just go from crisis to crisis, problem to problem. If you've got the perception but not the will, then you may as well not start on the route.
>
> But if you're in a traditional British company with incompetent foremen, militant shop stewards, a recalcitrant workforce, management that is out of touch – all the usual things – then you've got to start off with somebody, somewhere who says 'Hey, there must be a different way!'[2]

STRATEGIES: WHAT THEY ARE AND HOW THEY ARE FORMED

What they are

A strategy is a statement of intent which provides the basis for the implementation of plans. It is an explicit guide to the future behaviour required to achieve the mission and goals of the organization. Strategy defines the courses of action and allocation of resources required to reach these goals. Strategic thinking involves a deliberate and conscious choice of direction. As Rosabeth Moss Kanter writes:

> Strong leaders articulate direction and save the organization from change by drift. . . . They see a vision of the future that allows themselves and others to see more clearly the steps to take, building on present capacities and strengths.[3]

She believes that strategic plans 'elicit the present actions required for the future' and become 'action vehicles – integrating and institutionalizing mechanisms for change.'

How strategies are formed

In an ideal world, strategies would be formed by a deliberate process of analysis, diagnosis and prognosis. But it does not always happen like that.

Action precedes thought. Conflicts are converted to consensus. 'Accidents, uncertainties and muddle-headed confusions disappear into clear-sighted certainties. . . . Equally plausible alternatives disappear into obvious choices.'[4]

Henry Mintzberg suggests that strategies need not be deliberate. They can emerge. In theory, he says, strategy making is a systematic process. 'First we think, then we act. We formulate, then we implement.'[5] In practice, according to Mintzberg, 'a realized strategy can emerge in response to an evolving situation.' The strategist can often be 'a pattern organizer, a learner if you like, who manages a process in which strategies (and visions) can emerge as well as be deliberately conceived. . . . To manage strategy . . . is not so much to promote change as to *know* when to do so.'

Anyone who has sat on the board of a company knows that this concept of strategy as an evolving process is a correct one. Strategy emerges from events, even crises, and becomes the accepted course of direction although it has not been expressed in any formal planning document.

At Book Club Associates, for example, someone had the bright idea of breaking away from the core business of general book clubs and starting an Ancient History Club. It worked, and a strategy of segmentation emerged. No one said at a board meeting 'Let there be segmentation.' We sat and said 'Segmentation seems to be a good thing, let's do more of it.' And we did. The strategy, however, was articulated. Everyone understood that this was where the company was going.

It also had a strong influence on personnel strategy. We decided that segmentation was something that the whole management team had to be involved in. Two-day marketing conferences were held twice a year for all 50 senior managers from every department. We formed a new club development project team with representatives from each of the key departments which was chaired by the personnel director. The team initiated market research, prepared proposals, financial projections and a market entry plan, and supervised the launch. We did this not just to ensure that everyone concerned got involved in making it happen, but also as a deliberate means of improving teamwork and developing managers so that they had a deeper and a wider understanding of this new way of doing business and the contribution they could make to it. So, almost by accident, this became part of BCA's management development strategy.

STRATEGY AND THE CORPORATE PLAN

The word strategy is often used loosely as a synonym for any form of plan. It is more than that. A plan defines with some precision how an end result is to be attained. Strategies articulate the way forward to a desirable future state of being and provide the context within which action plans can be formed.

Strategies can be developed for the organization as a whole, for a major activity in the organization, such as marketing, or for a sub-activity, such as advertising. They can, and often are, formed quite independently in different parts of the organization. But to ensure that they are congruent with overall business strategy and contribute to it fully, corporate planning processes are used to integrate each part into the whole.

These processes will start with a definition of the mission of the organization, which includes an answer to the question 'What business are we in?' They will involve the definition of broadly defined goals and may include a swot analysis (the strengths and weaknesses of the organization and the opportunities and threats facing it). Goals will be amended as required on the basis of this analysis and strategies will then be defined for each part of the business.

Corporate planners provide guidelines and set out the assumptions to be made in developing strategies. They co-ordinate the process of preparing them so that they are fully integrated as a corporate plan. Corporate planning is almost always an iterative process. Proposals and ideas go backwards and forwards between functions and upwards and downwards between levels and are subject to modification at every stage to ensure that they form a cohesive whole in accord with the mission and goals of the organization.

A corporate planning system like this ensures that human resource considerations are taken into account during the process of planning rather than as an afterthought. This is the best way of getting personnel into the business and, therefore, into improving bottom-line performance.

These activities should not be over-formalized. Many highly successful companies do not produce a weighty corporate plan but they will still have gone through the processes and there will be a coherent strategy, even if it has not been expressed on reams of paper. The thing to do, as Alan Fell says:

> ... is to get the balance between a corporate plan which is substantial but is not a sub-industry in its own right. I have known organizations where the plan was so out of touch that no one understood it and it didn't mean anything.

And he went on to throw cold water over the pretentions some people have about corporate planning.

> Running a business is a whole multitude of mini-decisions, and you're involved in those. There aren't many macro-decisions. Some human resource people have this view that they will sit at some great corporate planning table and they will say that in 1999 we will be like this. It isn't like that, it really isn't like that. Most business is made up of contradictions, of backward movements, of forward movements, of absolute nonsenses, of irrationalities, of people screwing it up here, people screwing it up there. In reality, the situation is that if you've got it 60 per cent right, you are doing well. As a business you will grow. I have heard it said of one 'movie mogul' that if he had made all the films he had rejected and not made the films he had, he would be in exactly the same position.

What you have to avoid is the situation which Terry Murphy once lived with, in which his firm

> ... ran probably one of the most sophisticated business planning systems in the world. In fact it was so sophisticated that it almost became an end in itself rather than a means to an end.

These are salutary comments. No one, least of all personnel people, should believe that strategic planning is all-important. It can do no more, or less, than provide a sense of direction, which will help the firm to 'get it at least 60 per cent right'.

WHAT HUMAN RESOURCE STRATEGIES LOOK LIKE

Geoff Armstrong believes that plans for people should be:

- integral to business plans
- comprehensive
- bold, ambitious and forward-looking
- explicit
- related to business competitiveness
- communicated directly and continuously.

But that does not mean that they have to be grand, elaborate designs covering sheets of paper which nobody reads. The important thing is to provide an overall sense of purpose for the personnel activities of resourcing, organization planning and development, performance management, improving quality and gaining commitment. This helps people to understand where they are going, why certain things are happening and, most importantly, the contribution they are expected to make.

This is how Peter Hobbs sees it:

> It may take years to take initiatives in some companies, but when they finally take it, they completely understand what they are doing. This means that implementation is instantaneous. People tend to take decisions galore, but too often go through the process of acting without thinking and then, because they haven't prepared the ground, take years to sort out what the decision was about.
>
> I think what is crucial is that people do have a sense of where they are going. We need to tell them about our business objectives, we need to educate them widely in the ways in which our particular organization is going forward.

How it is done at Ford

John Hougham talks about how personnel strategies fit into the business plan at Ford.

We fully participate in a regular planning process which takes into account all the major components of the company. We start with contributions to the strategic review. There may be special contributions on issues which we believe are of particular importance in the year we are looking at, like the growth of information technology or any acquisitions. But more importantly, we are looking ahead and asking 'What is the outlook for the market?' Because after all that's what we are all here for. We are all here to make motor cars, and trucks and tractors and whatever, and sell them. So there is a tremendous amount of input from the sales and marketing people.

Then we get contributions from the manufacturing people. What kind of impact is new technology going to have on the business? What is the plan this year to continue improving quality? (This is paramount.) What do they see as being achievable in terms of further productivity improvements? And this process runs right through each facet of the business. When it comes to us the kind of things we are saying, they are about quality, the human dimension of quality – what are we doing to inculcate quality thinking into people, to make them more responsible for quality? We talk about our plans for improving the calibre of the workforce, our recruitment plans, what we are going to do about shortfalls, the demographic problem – there aren't going to be so many good people around, so what are we going to do about it? We discuss the need to interchange people more between the various parts of our business, manufacturing and engineering, to grow more rounded managers. We have started to talk about developing people much more between national companies, to grow good European managers.

We talk also on the issues that manufacturing, sales and marketing have highlighted, because none of these things stands in isolation. We say what we think we in personnel should be doing to respond to those requirements and, by the way, here are some ideas of our own. We talk about compensation strategy – 'Fordspeak' for how you pay people and what benefits they have – bringing the executive up to date on what's going on in the outside world, profit-sharing, relating pay to performance, for example.

And then we look at labour strategy – recognizing that what we are really after is increasing flexibility, with less demarcation. What is the likely union reaction going to be to that?

The Cadbury Schweppes approach

The planning process at corporate level in Cadbury Schweppes was described by Peter Reay as follows:

> All our businesses produce their individual business plans which are aggregated and synthesized at corporate level. We extract from that the key issues which the group of Cadbury Schweppes has to address so that the executive board can discuss strategic priorities, the great majority of which are about growth.
>
> It was quite clear that underpinning all of them was the issue of management resource, so that became an additional strategic question: did we have the right people of the right quality to develop the business along the lines we wanted?

The Coopers & Lybrand approach

Mike Stanton stressed that at Coopers & Lybrand the human resource plan had to be part of the corporate plan:

> We have to do this in consultancy because our only resource is people. We make a forward market projection that says it looks as if we will get a bigger market share, or go into new markets, or whatever. You then immediately look at the implications of this in terms of the numbers of people required and the rate at which you are likely to be able to get them. And this could be a constraint on your rate of growth.

The Thorn EMI approach

In the nature of things, human resource strategies have generally to be broad brush affairs which point the way to go but are not explicit about how to get there. This is a perfectly proper approach. It means that detailed planning can take place within a defined framework, but there is still scope to flex the plans to meet changing circumstances. Strategy is a living thing, it cannot be frozen.

The Thorn EMI approach, as outlined by Don Young, was first of all to define the following five main characteristics of the group:

1   Its capacity to manage businesses in different national markets and exploit its creative/marketing and technological and management skills internationally;

2   Its ability to give real opportunity and authority for strong managers to be enterprising in their own businesses, whilst exercising strong strategic control through the willingness of its top management to behave interdependently;

3 Its ability to co-ordinate its approaches fast and responsively to market opportunities which require integrated action by more than one business area;

4 Having a strong balance between demanding excellence of performance from its managers and investing humanity, skill and time into helping managers to improve their performance and potential;

5 Its ability to manage its research and technologies in a market sensitive manner.

Strategic priorities could then be determined for the development of an organization which would strongly manifest these characteristics.

The TSB approach

Nick Cowan explained that:

> We use our management committee, one of our top committees, as the management development committee. This enables us to integrate management development with our strategic planning, which is essential because so much of what we do depends on having people with the right skills and capabilities. You can't do management development unless you know what you are developing for. The strategic planning process brings these dimensions together.

The Book Club Associates approach

BCA starts its corporate planning process with an 'away day' for members of the executive board. This is a free-wheeling affair. the only formal input is usually a presentation by an economist from the Henley Forecasting Centre on economic, political and social trends as they will affect BCA's business. In the light of this, the meeting constructs scenarios of the future state of BCA. Broad business goals are derived from these which are, of course, mainly concerned with the marketing strategies needed to reach acceptable targets for growth and profitability. All members of the board, including the personnel director, are expected to make an equal contribution to this debate. Naturally each will look at things from the perspective of his or her own function and the factors in that area which must be taken into account. But functional interest is subordinated to corporate needs.

A SWOT analysis (strengths and weaknesses, opportunities and threats) is also carried out. This will specifically include the human resource aspect so that, if there are any potential constraints in that area, plans can be made to deal with them.

Finally a look is taken at the company's mission statement, which includes a 'what business are we in' definition, and revisions made as necessary. The latest statement emphasized equally the business and the people aspects:

> Book Club Associates is in the business of the direct marketing and supply of in-house leisure products for the purposes of entertainment, education and self-improvement.
>
> BCA earns its living in a competitive world and it needs to compete successfully to meet its obligations to all those who have a stake in the business – its owners and the people who work there.
>
> The basis of our enterprise is the goodwill of our customers – the members who join our bookclubs and those who buy from our catalogues. We are in business to identify and meet their needs.
>
> The success of BCA ultimately depends upon the quality and commitment of its people. BCA believes in providing individuals with opportunities to make the best of their abilities and to grow with the firm. We also believe that openness, trust and fair treatment are the basis of the good working relationships upon which the effectiveness of the organization depends.
>
> Our standards are demanding but we appreciate that demanding standards require appropriate rewards.

The 'away day' produces broad guidelines as a skeleton for the corporate plan. Some flesh is put on this skeleton by the finance and operation research department. The latter has a suite of business models which it can use to project future results and resource requirements (including people) on the basis of certain assumptions. 'What if' questions can be answered and sensitivity analysis carried out to explore the profit implications of different assumptions.

Each function then prepares its own section of the plan. The human resource contribution concentrates on organizational, resourcing, performance and industrial relations issues and strategies.

The sectional plans are then co-ordinated by the director responsible for corporate planning and reviewed by the chief executive who, with the help of the planning director, writes the general, corporate, section of the plan.

The draft plan is next discussed by the board and an iterative process is embarked upon to produce an agreed plan at this level. This is then presented to the 50 senior managers of the company at another 'away day'. In one way or another, most of these will have been involved in preparing parts of the plan, but this conference gives them the opportunity to hear about the whole plan and to make comments on it, which are listened to and acted upon.

The corporate planning process in itself was part of the human resource strategy and was developed and run as such by the writer. Not only did it help to integrate the different functions of BCA but it was also used to increase the commitment of directors, managers and staff to the achievement of the company's mission, bearing in mind that it is people who ultimately implement the corporate plan.

References

1   DRUCKER, Peter. *Managing for results*. London, Heinemann, 1964
2   WICKENS, Peter, *The road to Nissan*. London, Macmillan, 1987
3   KANTER, Rosabeth Moss. *The change masters*. London, Allen & Unwin, 1984
4   *Ibid*.
5   MINTZBERG, Henry. 'Crafting strategy'. *Harvard Business Review*, July/August 1987, pp 66–73

9 Corporate Culture and the Bottom Line

WHAT IS CORPORATE CULTURE?

Corporate culture is the pattern of shared attitudes, beliefs, assumptions and expectations which shape the way people act and interact in an organization and underpin the way that things get done.

Corporate culture encompasses the norms and core values of an enterprise and manifests itself in the form of organization climate, management style, organization behaviour, or 'the way things are done around here' and the structure and systems of the organization.

Norms

Norms are the unwritten rules of behaviour which strongly influence climate, management style and how people work together, conduct themselves and carry out their tasks.

The norms of an organization may, for example, produce behaviour which is relaxed and friendly. There is a lot of informal chat (perhaps too much), walking about, drifting in and out of offices, and *ad hoc* meetings which may often appear to be inconclusive but which still get things done. Alternatively, the norms may result in behaviour where relationships are formalized, distances are maintained between levels, meetings are highly structured and everything is recorded on paper.

Core values

Core values are the basic beliefs about what is good or best for the organization, and about what management thinks is important, what should or should not happen. There will be a value system or set which will be accepted by management who will say, in effect, these are the things we believe are important. The core values may or may not be expressed

103

formally in a value statement, and this may or may not be shared or accepted by the members of the organization.

Core values can refer to:

- care and consideration for people

- care for customers

- competitiveness

- enterprise

- excellence

- flexibility

- growth as a major objective

- innovation

- market/customer orientation

- performance orientation

- productivity

- quality

- teamwork.

These values are often formulated as a management statement, sometimes backed up by lists of general principles on how they should be applied.

Values should be distinguished from norms. Values express judgements about what sorts of behaviour are considered desirable and worthwhile and what sorts are not. Norms do not contain such judgements. They simply exist, having been formed by custom and practice, which may be good, bad or indifferent. To shift norms people have to learn and practise new forms of behaviour and these may take time to sink in and effect a permanent change. To get people to adopt new behaviour patterns it may be necessary to persuade them to accept different values and reinforce that process with suitable training.

This is often attempted by adopting a top-down approach. Values are formulated at board level and are then communicated to everybody by means of booklets and briefings. To try to obtain commitment to the values, workshop or training events will be held throughout the organization. These workshops will aim to inculcate the values and to educate those attending in the application of the general principles.

A bottom-up approach to the development of shared values would start with an analysis of the existing value sets of employers through 'focus groups' (small groups of employees who discuss issues related to values), broader, unstructured group discussions, attitude surveys, questionnaires and interviews. These reveal attitudes, beliefs and norms.

Through further discussions at all levels, these can be articulated as values which are eventually incorporated into a statement endorsed by the chief executive and the board. Clearly the latter will have been involved in the debate and will want to influence the formulation of the values. The bottom-up approach therefore requires a degree of iteration – further discussions at all levels about the emerging value set as effected by deliberations at the top. The bottom-up approach is elaborate and time-consuming but it is the best way not only to share values but also to get people to 'own' them.

There is no one right way of developing shared values and commitment to them. It is hard work, whichever way it is carried out. If done properly, however, it can make a significant impact on organizational performance and the bottom line by influencing behaviour in directions which are most likely to achieve the results the organization wants.

Value statements are most likely to be effective if they are prepared along the following lines:

- the values espoused by management should be in accordance with the actual norms, climate, management style and patterns of behaviour in the organization; if they are not, steps should be taken to bring them into line;

- as far as possible the values should be developed in conjunction with all concerned, although management and, indeed, any member of the organization can provide leads;

- the chief executive must put all his or her weight behind the programmes for developing the statement of values and for obtaining commitment to them;

- the programme for obtaining commitment should be a continuous one – it should not rely on the fact that the value statement was produced jointly by management and staff;

- the commitment programme should include workshops as well as more formal courses in any skills required to implement the general principles;

- it should be understood that the best way to change values and gain their acceptance is to influence behaviour at all levels; values are formed by behaviour but at the same time can exert influence over it;

- values need reinforcing by maintaining appropriate behaviour, by follow-up workshops and, importantly, by rewarding behaviour which supports the values and by indicating disapproval of unsupportive behaviour.

Organization climate

Organization climate is the working atmosphere of the organization as perceived by its members. It is shaped and influenced by norms, values and the behaviour of the chief executive and managers, which sets the 'tone' of the organization. And the key player is, of course, the chief executive, who can have an enormous influence on the climate, for good or for ill.

The climate will be characterized by features such as these:

- adaptive or unchangeable
- flexible or rigid
- pro-active or reactive
- fluid or bureaucratic
- unstructured or hierarchical
- innovative or staid
- results orientated or production/maintenance orientated
- expansionist or restrictive
- forceful or *laissez-faire*
- profit emphasis or cost control emphasis
- people orientated or task orientated
- process bias or systems bias
- apolitical or political
- relaxed or stressful
- co-operataive or combative
- team approach or individual approach
- friendly or hostile
- informal or formal
- open or closed (communications)
- free and easy or status conscious
- quality as a way of life or lack of concern
- focus on customers or internal focus.

Management style

Management style describes the way in which managers set about achieving results through people. It is how managers behave as team leaders and how they exercise authority. Managers can be autocratic or democratic, tough or soft, demanding or easy-going, directive or *laissez-faire*, distant or accessible, destructive or supportive, task orientated or people orientated, rigid or flexible, considerate or unfeeling, friendly or cold, keyed up or relaxed. How they behave will depend partly on themselves – their natural inclinations, partly on the example given to them by their managers, and partly on the norms, values and climate of the organization.

Management style can be influenced by counselling, coaching and training. The best way of exerting influence, however, is to help managers to understand what their styles are (most people have more than one, which they use in different situations) and how they can adapt their natural style as required to become more effective. There are a number of instruments or self-completion questionnaires such as LIFO (life orientation) which can be used for the purpose. Team building and interactive skills training can also make managers more aware of what is productive and unproductive about their styles so that they can work out for themselves how to improve.

Organization behaviour

Organization behaviour is the way in which people act in the organization, individually or in groups. This embraces the extent to which they are motivated, committed, indifferent, co-operative, intractable, energetic or lethargic. It also includes the various processes in the organization such as planning, innovating, coping with change, delegating, co-operating, involving, interacting, communicating, measuring, appraising and rewarding.

These processes will critically affect the way things get done and the results achieved. They will be strongly influenced by the other aspects of corporate culture: norms, values, climate and management style. Culture management programmes aim either to maintain effective behaviour or to change dysfunctional behaviour. They do this by working on values and management style but also by various interventions to help people understand where they are going and to identify areas and methods for improvement. These may include various forms of workshops as used in organization development programmes.

Organizational processes are also affected by the various personnel systems used in the organization, particularly those concerned with performance management, objective setting, appraisal, coaching, counselling and rewards. The performance review and reward management systems can be used to convey messages about what is regarded as appropriate or inappropriate behaviour and thus reinforce the former and indicate the steps required to overcome the latter.

Structure and systems

Corporate culture will affect the ways in which the organization is structured and operated. These will include the amount of rigidity or flexibility allowed in the structure, the extent to which informal processes of interaction and communication override or replace formal channels, the amount of authority that is devolved from the top or the centre, and the degree to which jobs are compartmentalized and rigidly defined. It may affect the number of layers of management, the spans of control of managers and the extent to which decisions are made by teams rather than by individuals.

The development and use of systems will also be affected by the corporate culture and will in turn help to shape it. A bureaucratic or mechanistic organization will attempt to govern everything through systems or manuals. An organic approach will only allow systems which are functions of the situation in which the enterprise finds itself rather than conforming to any pre-determined and rigid view of how it should operate. In some organizations, people follow systems to the letter, in others, people take pride in 'bucking the system' and cutting corners to get things done. Systems can be used as control mechanisms to enforce conformity or they can be flexed to allow scope for responding to new situations as they arise.

Why is corporate culture relevant?

Corporate culture is relevant to the bottom line simply because it is instrumental in directing the energies of the members of the organization towards the achievement of its objectives. And these objectives in any business must incorporate growth, survival, innovation, competitive edge, added value and profit

Organization culture is important because it is both a source of strength and, potentially, a critical constraint on business strategy. It is a key concept for personnel managers because, first, it is created by and impacts on people and, secondly, the organization's human resource strategies, processes and practices can create, enhance or undermine its culture.

A word of caution

Corporate culture is deep and pervasive and cannot be changed quickly. There is no evidence that organizational success is in any way related to cultural strength or cultural type. There are no such things as right or wrong cultures. There are only relevant or irrelevant ones. And relevance is a function of the degree to which the culture enables or hinders the organization to achieve its objectives.

Culture management as a lever for change

The pursuit of improved bottom-line performance means that most organizations are in a constant state of self-generated change. Simultaneously they have to manage the change imposed upon them by their external environment.

In these circumstances, functional cultures – that is, those which support the achievement of the organization's aims – have to be preserved. This will happen naturally if they are adaptive and continue to operate effectively under pressure. If this is not the case, steps may have to be taken to preserve the culture. Coherence and unity of purpose may have to be maintained by explaining to everyone what is happening, why it is happening and how they can help to make it happen.

A more usual situation is that the culture has to be changed to help the organization to meet new challenges, to exploit new opportunities, to achieve significant improvements in performance, to manage turbulence, to absorb new technology, to introduce new products, to develop new markets or to beat off a threat.

But it is not simply a matter of changing the culture under pressure. Culture management processes can be used as levers for change, to ensure that the organization moves purposefully towards where it wants to go. This clearly constitutes the most positive use of corporate culture and the rest of this chapter therefore concentrates on cultural change programmes.

WHAT IS CULTURE CHANGE?

Culture change is the process of shaping or re-shaping the culture of an organization in order to improve its performance and to help it manage and benefit from changes in its environment, its markets, its ownership, its leadership, its products or its technology.

A culture change programme aims to modify or reconstruct norms, values, attitudes and beliefs in order to encourage different or new behaviours which will contribute to the achievement of the goals of the enterprise.

Ultimately, however, the aim of a cultural change programme is to enable the organization to achieve its goals as developed from its mission and strategy.

The change process

A change programme should incorporate the following processes as suggested by Richard Beckhard[1]:

- setting goals and defining the future state or organizational conditions desired after the change;

- diagnosing the present condition in relation to those goals;

- defining the transition state activities and commitments required to meet the future state;

- developing strategies and action plans for managing this transition.

The cultural change programme

Cultural change programmes consist of the following stages:

1   Setting broad objectives and goals for the programme in terms of specified improvements in organizational performance. These objectives would be based on an analysis of the strategy and goals of the organization.

2   Further analysis in the light of these objectives of:

- the existing culture. What are the core values? What is the organization climate? What are the typical behaviour patterns and norms?

- the changes taking place to or within the organization now and in the future; the mission and goals of the enterprise.

3   Diagnosis of the relevance of the existing culture and its capacity to help or hinder the organization to manage change and to achieve its objectives.

4   Decisions in the light of the analysis and diagnosis of the extent to which culture change is necessary to achieve improvements in areas such as:

- overall commitment to the organization's values and goals
- entrepreneurial activity and innovation
- market orientation
- profit consciousness
- cost consciousness
- results orientation
- quality
- customer care and service
- productivity.

5   Definition or re-definition of the company's mission statement and statement of core values. The benefits and methods of doing this would have to be carefully considered. It would be necessary to ensure so far as possible that the statements:

- represent what is actually happening or express intentions that, demonstrably, will be made to happen;

- have personality, in other words, reflect what the organization and its management are really like and are not bland pieces of prose reached down from the shelf;

- are based on top management consensus about their content and message;

- are formulated hand in hand with the definition of objectives, strategies, critical success factors and performance criteria – where the business intends to go, how it intends to get there and how it will know it has arrived at its destination.

6   Articulation and dissemination of an agenda for change – what the management wants to do and why, and how it wants it to happen. this agenda can be built round the mission statement, the statement of core values and the declared goals and strategies of the organization.

7   Formulation, planning and implementation of a culture change programme designed to achieve objectives as articulated in the agenda for change. The change programme would be designed to get the message

across and ensure, so far as possible, that it is understood, accepted and acted upon.

8 Measuring the change programme against its objectives to ensure that it is going according to plan.

Change strategies
The methods to be considered in a cultural change programme would include, depending on the circumstances, a choice of one or more of the following change strategies:

- The issue to all concerned of the agenda for change and the statements of mission and values. By itself this strategy would almost certainly fail. It has to be replaced or supported by other approaches.

- Personal briefings on the proposed changes cascading down through the organization using such mechanisms as team briefing. This is better than simply issuing pieces of paper but may still result in a 'so what' reaction.

- Workshops in which groups get together to discuss, analyze and interpret the proposed changes and any mission and value statements. These can be useful if they cover each level, if ample scope is given for representing the proposals in language and actions appropriate to the individuals or groups concerned (as long as their essence remains) and if follow-up action is taken.

- Various forms of educational or training programmes which allow plenty of time to get the various messages across and to discuss their meaning and application fully. British Airways' 'Putting People First' is an example of this sort of programme which involved all 38,000 staff attending an intensive three-day workshop encouraging them to think about and accept the importance of customer service.

- Performance management programmes which ensure through the mechanisms of objective and target setting, performance appraisal and review, counselling and coaching that the values, norms and behaviours which the cultural change programme is developing are absorbed and acted upon as part of the normal process of management.

- Reward management processes which ensure that people are rewarded for behaviour which is in accord with the values and aims of the culture change programme and are punished or at least helped to see the error of their ways if their behaviour is inappropriate.

- Intensive quality improvement programmes which specifically develop attitudes and behaviours designed to enhance the quality of the product or service marketed by the organization, and provide added value to customers.

- Customer care programmes designed to improve customer awareness and levels of service.

- Resourcing policies which recruit, develop and promote people who 'fit' the desired culture of the organization.

- Communication and involvement programmes using media and processes such as joint consultation, team briefing, quality circles and joint task forces to reinforce and generate commitment to the message, and to get things moving.

Requirements for success

Cultural change programmes only succeed if they are led from the top and are perceived by everyone concerned as representing the vision and values of the chief executive. As Rosabeth Moss Kanter wrote:

> The skill of corporate leaders, the ultimate change masters, lies in their ability to envision a new reality and aid in its translation into concrete terms.[2]

Only with this sort of leadership can the organization achieve its 'culture of pride and climate of success'.

The leader articulates the mission and defines the agenda but he or she needs help to launch and run the culture change programme. And this is where the personnel function can or should play a major part.

As Peter Reay of Cadbury Schweppes remarked, cultural change is an

> ... issue where the personnel function has a distinctive contribution to make. Not only are we heavily involved in recruitment, training and development, we are also involved in giving advice about organization structure, compensation incentives and, very importantly, all aspects of communication. What we are actually about in doing these things is changing the culture in order to achieve much more demanding business objectives.

And Len Peach said that:

> I am a great believer in personnel management as a change agent in the business of creating and revising policy and influencing behaviour. In the case of the National Health Service management, it does not have a clear view of what its role is in relation to its employees. So it's a matter of pioneering, trying to build up a series of policies which in the end will create the environment you need.

Mike Stanton thought that:

> We have a lot to offer, we personnel people, in managing the process of change. We have to get through to the board that the leadership of the change process has to come through line management. Thereafter, making it happen is about conditioning,

guiding the perceptions and modifying the attitudes and behaviour of management from the top down. This involves running the actual processes that make it happen: workshops, training programmes, whatever. It means deciding whether to do it top down, bottom up or both. It means monitoring to assess how the change is happening, modifying the appraisal scheme so that people are set appropriate objectives, coaching people so that they work with the set of values the company wants, developing pay structures which reinforce the values you want and all the rest of it.

But he also issued some words of warning:

The first thing to beware of is the notion of culture change. I think that while corporate culture is very important, one doesn't necessarily always have to be changing it. But at least one has to appraise it, integrate it and ensure that it is right and is working. This is simply because organizations are dynamic things, they are always in a state of change. So the structure constantly needs to change and the 'dynamic' constantly needs to be appraised and developed. By the dynamic, I mean the things that make the organization tick, the informal organization, the ways in which people behave, their attitudes around the place, their motivation.

I think the best definition of corporate culture, apart from the sort of everyday definition of 'the way we do things around here', is that it is the set of values, attitudes and beliefs which, in the absence of other direct instructions, guide people in their everyday work. These can work to the benefit of the organization in the sense of delivering its goals: profit, service to customer, quality and so on. And they are to a certain extent manipulable. There are lots of organizations which have quite consciously set out to engender a particular attitude of mind. IBM is a classic case, also Hewlett Packard and Digital.

I do think that one has to maintain, modify and nurture the culture and the personnel function provides the professional tools to do it.

A recent study we've been involved in demonstrates that culture change programmes are not generated by personnel people. They nearly always arise because of a new chief executive or some step changes in the organization like a merger, an acquisition or loss of a major part of the business. These latter force change on the chief executive. Very rarely do personnel people push this and, if they do, they do it through the chief executive. What personnel people can do very effectively is to ask the questions which force the board and line management to think through all of the corporate culture issues. Directors need help to think about what kind of culture they want. They're often very misty about it, and it's very difficult. It takes an awful lot of work to get straight the definition of what we want to be like, not just our mission, but all the values we want to abide by.

The personnel department can provide technical help at a high level by assessing what the starting point is and by establishing what the current values and beliefs are, using attitude surveys, for example.

Tony Vineall is also cautious about being too starry-eyed about cultural change but does believe in the contribution the personnel function can make:

It's difficult to make sensible statements about corporate culture. It always seems to me that the people who do try and talk about it as if it were a very quantifiable thing tend to overdo it. Accordingly I often feel slightly uncomfortable when people talk about changing the culture in this way or that. But in the end that is what we're after. . . . There's no stopping a business if you've got people's commitment, when they feel that if they get stuck in, the pay-off to them will be commensurate, that there will be opportunities for them and money for them.

Culture is to a great extent determined by key events and a lot of these key events relate to people. Personnel can therefore exert influence on the culture by encouraging an imaginative allocation of responsibility to somebody.

I think cultures are influenced by people events, by events in their working lives. And I think that to exert influence on these events personnel people have to be able to see beyond the rules.

Personnel people can often affect the climate and the culture by getting the right debate to happen at the right time. At certain times of frustration in an organization or at points where everybody's going through difficult times, you can sometimes organize an event where everyone takes time out to think. You can often hear people talk about the Torquay conference or the Maidenhead meeting as a time, not when you made a major change and came round a corner, but when you became crucially conscious that you were going round a corner.

I believe they're enormously valuable but it's difficult to get them right because personnel managers are not popular if they are forever asking to have conferences. But the right one at the right time can work. They can really influence the culture by providing space for management to think about things. so one should at least try sometimes to persuade the organization to take a day out, perhaps a weekend, and go away somewhere.

In Don Beattie's view, the contribution of the personnel function to culture change is to ask such questions as:

What sort of place do we need to be? What is our value system? What underpinning policies and practices do we need which are not totally disfunctional to that value system? If you have policies pointing in one direction and a cultural statement pointing in that direction, you're not going to go very far. They've got to be aligned, and they've got to be saying the same sort of things, albeit to different levels and in different words and for different audiences. So you need to get policy, culture, process, behaviour and attitude lined up behind where you want the organization to be in five years time.

It's very tough to change an organization if the vision is not there in the chief executive. To an extent you can create the vision but he's got to believe and actually communicate pretty vigorously the sort of company it needs to be.

Don Beattie is quite certain that culture change programmes are necessary from his own experience in ICL (summarized as a case history in the last section of this chapter, see page 121):

We are undergoing a dramatically rapid rate of change in this business. So how do you get the organization to change? I always see it like a shoal of fish swimming. You know how fish can suddenly just turn through 90 degrees all together – and they're all going in the same direction? One of the tricks for us, I think, is to get an organization that can do that – an organization of 30 to 35,000 people. We don't need to turn the whole of it at once, but we should certainly try to get 25 to 30,000 of it to move. We just have to say: 'Hey, hang on everyone, not that direction, we've got to turn!', and it moves. And that's terribly important in rapid change. You've got to be able to track the market and if your tail is three years behind your head, you've got a business which is not going to make any change at all in the marketplace.

Peter Hobbs of Wellcome suggests that the following approach to cultural change is necessary:

You must have some star or planet which is on your mind as defining what to go for. And you get as many people as you can to share that vision. The route you use to get there is wholly pragmatic. It may well involve steps backwards as well as steps forward. The important thing is to achieve, as far as you can, a shared view of where you are going. This is certainly true in quality terms and, to a lesser extent, in quantity terms. You may have a vision in your organization that you are going to be the biggest printer and therefore destroyer of forests in the world. But how you get there will involve many material considerations in terms of the people and equipment you want. The means change all the time: governments intervene with pay freezes, factories blow up, demography says that there won't be enough people around. But the vision, the shared view, remains as the guiding star.

Limitations to cultural change programmes
Cultural change, as Ed Schein says:

> ... is a long painful process. How it is managed and what is needed depends on the stage reached by the organization, the industry, technological forces, national culture and available leadership.[3]

Cultural assumptions can become barriers to necessary change and removing these barriers is not always an easily or quickly accomplished task. As Don Beattie says from his experience in running the ICL change programme:

> I've always said that culture change is a 15-year programme, and that may be optimistic. It's certainly a long haul.

When and when not to introduce a corporate change programme
Deal and Kennedy say that there are only five reasons to justify large-scale cultural change programmes[4]:

1 If your company has strong values that do not fit a changing environment;

2 If the industry is very competitive and moves with lightning speed;

3 If your company is mediocre or worse;

4 If your company is about to join the ranks of the very largest companies;

5 If your company is small but growing rapidly.

Deal and Kennedy say that if none of these reasons apply, don't do it. Their analysis of 10 cases of attempted cultural change indicated that it will cost between five and 10 per cent of what you already spend on the people whose behaviour is supposed to change and even then you are likely to get only half the improvement you want. They warn that it costs a lot (in time, effort and money) and will take a long time.

The way ahead
Culture change is, as Don Beattie said, a long haul. But you often have no choice but to embark on it if the organization is going to survive and thrive. Good and effective cultures need to be preserved and nurtured, ineffective ones need to be re-shaped. But culture is a somewhat amorphous concept and culture change programmes can seem to be abstract and unreal. The rest of this chapter is therefore devoted to descriptions of culture change programmes which, it is hoped, will make the concept come to life.

Abbey National

Terry Murphy describes the cultural change programme at Abbey National.

How does one begin? Well, we started very simply by sitting down with the general manager's team and defining the very straightforward things such as: the sort of business we were, the sort of business we thought we should have in the new financial services environment, the sort of posture in the market we should take, the sort of business shape we could envisage in the long-term future – but it takes a long time.

That process took us about four to five months, but we developed some very clear ideas about what the possibilities were. We had seen the reports which we knew would form the basis of government thinking about the role building societies should fill. We also took a lot of information on board about the way in which financial services markets were changing, not only in the UK but worldwide, because inevitably the UK market is going to reflect what is happening in the rest of the world. So by that stage we had developed a feeling of what sort of business we were and what sort of business we wanted to be.

It was pretty evident that one of the prime requirements was to change the nature and culture of the organization. It just didn't fit. We had a totally uncommercial culture. Profit was a meaningless concept. You didn't need it. The Building Societies Association decided the rates, so once they had done that the margins were decided, and the only determination of profit was your costs. So all you needed to worry about was controlling costs.

It became our belief that we needed to change pretty significantly. We needed to generate, in effect, a performance-orientated organization.

This meant that we had to prepare the organization for change by the way in which we used language, by the way in which we managed the organization for the sort of culture we wanted to create. This is critical because if you don't communicate using the right sort of language and adopt the right sort of behaviour then you have no chance of changing other people's aspirations or behaviour.

What we also needed to do was to develop a human resource posture where what we did was much more tightly linked with the organization's behaviour – what it wanted to achieve.

We then put together the culture change programme which was basically a training extension but was supported by changes in management style, by changes in policy and by changes in procedures; and these were very significant.

Cadbury Schweppes

As Peter Reay explained:

> The main thing that has been happening in our business has been change over the last four or five years at an ever accelerating pace. Change is basically about changing people, sometimes literally, getting better people in place of ones who aren't so effective . . . !
>
> I don't think there are any simple cookbook solutions to organizational and structural change. In a sense you have to trade very heavily upon your knowledge of the business, your knowledge of the people in the business, your feel for what is going to work in terms of delivering results. Your claim for a distinctive contribution tends to depend upon those things which you have learned within the business. Reading a textbook doesn't do me much good, actually.

Cadbury Schweppes does, however, have a very strongly defined approach to cultural change, as is indicated by the following paper produced by a project group set up to consider the implications of change.

Background
In developing a charter, the group felt that the most competitive advantage would be achieved by merging and integrating our policies; by identifying opportunities and addressing areas of current weakness across the different aspects of change. The group therefore first reviewed those different types of change currently seen across our various companies and in different countries of the Cadbury Schweppes world.
  These were:

1 *Business and market change.* In recent years there have been some significant changes in our various marketplaces, with significant shifts in our retail structures. At the same time we have set ourself more challenging targets for growth, market share and new product development. Inside our companies, whether in drinks, confectionery or foods, we have sought much needed increases in productivity, profitability and return on new capital investment. These programmes have required increased attention to employee communications.

2 *Technological change.* New technology, higher technology and information technology have hit the food and drink industry. It has brought with it new machinery and new methods – the need for higher skills and more flexibility in areas of management, craft and operator employment. Training for change will be critical in achieving competitive advantage.

3 *Structural change.* This is very topical in Cadbury Schweppes at the highest and lower levels. The shape of our business is changing and the effects reverberate throughout. Streaming and joint ventures, acquisi-

tion and divestment have become facts of life during recent months and years.

Further down our companies we have sought opportunities to review the structure of our operations for maximum effectiveness. Some operations and services have been contracted out to local profit centres with smaller locally-led working groups.

4 *Organization change – the people in our structures*. We are seeing change and innovation as we seek responsiveness and effective use of resources. For some years we have seen fewer jobs, fewer people, different working groups and shift systems. We are now moving from the quantitative to the qualitative approach to organization design.

5 *Procedure change – different ways of doing things*. Around the Cadbury Schweppes world we have seen change in our central business systems, change too in the relationships with our people.

6 *Cultural change – changing old-fashioned attitudes and beliefs*. There are predators around, and in different Cadbury countries we are seeing a need to be faster on our feet. Employees are adapting and contributing, and trade unions adapting and participating.

7 *Behavioural change – changing expectations but facilitating sharing in success*. Change demands better appreciation of the economic facts of life. Management styles are changing within our world but the leadership challenge remains critical to the achievement of change in manufacturing and commercial areas.

Objectives
The following objectives are those affecting the area of employee involvement which will enable Cadbury Schweppes to meet the challenges of the future.

1 To produce the highest quality product at the lowest cost in line with changing business and market conditions and ensuring a continuing competitive advantage.

2 To explore, evaluate and capitalize each distribution opportunity while continuing to operate in the most cost-effective system to sustain long-term growth.

3 To develop the employee business link through the establishment of open communication systems that ensure employees understand and are committed to business goals and performance.

4 To create and maintain an environment which develops and nurtures long-term employee commitment.

5 To develop an organization which encourages a participative management style.

6 To review and critically evaluate all of the traditional conditions of

employment and management practices, modifying those accordingly to achieve high quality results.

7 To provide direction and support to employee groups that enables those groups to initiate, adapt and accept new ideas and technology for continued profitable business growth.

8 To develop a management profile which encourages a participative leadership style embracing the organization's values and continuing to improve overall company performance.

Ford

John Hougham describes how, at Ford, change gave the personnel function 'a well-defined role as part of the business plan':

> There was a time when, in a sense, we did operate almost within closed walls but there was a factor that changed all that, and that factor was called survival. The major change came about in the middle 70s. One of our senior vice-presidents went to Japan and when he came back what he had seen turned into a programme which became known as 'after Japan'. And I don't think it's fanciful to say that we tend to date modern Ford in years 'AJ'.
>
> What it was all about was: 'This is what the Japanese are doing. I've seen it for myself. You had better believe that unless we start really getting our act together and becoming more efficient, more productive, more competitive, and all these other things, we will not survive.' It was that sort of stark message.
>
> This trip generated a whole series of action programmes which permeated the organization. But because a large part was directed to improving efficiency, improving productivity and therefore, slimming the company down dramatically, it was seen that just about all these programmes were going to have a dramatic effect on people – the human resource.
>
> At this point, I think I can say that, personnel and personnel planning became central to the business plan. It would probably be incorrect to say that we went from one day when nobody took any notice of the personnel department, to becoming central. But if I had to say there was a central point, then that was it. There was a catalyst at work and that catalyst was called survival. The catalyst was called: 'We've got to get into this people business and become efficient, productive and all the rest of it. And what are you – the personnel people – going to do to help us do that?'
>
> One of the things we did, was making that message known, because we all recognized the urgent need to become much better at communicating the business facts of life. Communica-

tion doesn't necessarily reside as the responsibility of the personnel department – all sorts of different people share it. But it is certainly our job to carry that message to the national trade union level when we are dealing with policy and making them aware of what was driving our programme. So we became very much involved in a number of presentations where a very senior team indeed – mainly manufacturing folk – went on the stomp all round Europe, setting out in open-book terms what we had to do to survive: business realities, including some pretty hard facts about the human resource.

IBM

IBM is well known for its very positively defined corporate culture. This is based on the following three principles (basic beliefs):

- respect for the individual;
- service to the customer;
- excellence must be a way of life.

Len Peach referred to the change process at IBM as follows:

It would be easier to describe change in IBM as fine tuning rather than radical change. In fact IBM is consistently, continuously changing, that's the beauty of the company. Occasionally it will go through violent change but on the whole it's evolutionary change. And the tenets remain the same.

This is in contrast to what happens in most other companies. People feel insecure and insecurity is a very good reason for resisting change.

Gordon Sapsed of IBM suggested that:

IBM changes everything except its basic beliefs. It strives to build values and get them accepted. All IBM managers regularly get together and spend a day brainstorming about what those beliefs and values mean. They are expected, indeed they are required, to look at them in the light of current goals and say: 'Hey, how does that affect us?'

ICL

Mission statement
The approach was based on a new mission for the company implying significant changes in direction. This was defined as:

ICL is an international company dedicated to applying information technology to providing profitable high-value customer solutions for operational and management effectiveness.

Key strategies

Objectives were set which were designed to build strength as a major European player in information technology, to focus on specific markets and to be known as a systems integrator with a reputation for quality.

The key strategies were to be built around:

- high-value solutions to defined markets
- commitment to open systems – providing customers with greater flexibility in the choice of manufacturer and with confidence for the future
- collaborations – to gain market or technical leverage
- organizational responsiveness – to react to the fast-changing market
- focus on systems and solutions for customers and on providing real added value for them in running their business.

Background to the cultural change programme

The background to ICL's cultural change programme was provided by the new managing director who said:

> I gradually realized that I lacked the levers to transfer my strategic insight into the hearts and minds of the organization so that they shared the imperative. They had to know *why*, not just *what*. An impressive programme of communication was not enough. I got immensely frustrated – thousands of bright people all working hard but not buying in to the direction.

He is also reported as having used the well-worn Second World War saying of a US general: 'I have seen the enemy, and he is us.'

He came to the conclusion that the ICL 'culture' was going to beat him if he did not do something. He had to change that culture, and integrate the company's strategic thinking with an organization capability that could match the challenges of the changes needed. In other words, part of his business strategy for change had to be in the development of the thinking and capability of the management group, and in resetting the cultural values of the organization.

The ICL Way

So what was the nature of the initiatives taken? In 1981, ICL had no common statement of its values and beliefs, and a number of sub-cultures.

There was the need for an explicit and common statment. In 1982 such a statement was prepared and fully publicized to all staff – entitled 'The ICL Way'. On the front cover was the statement 'The way we do things around here'. Inside were a set of commitments for all staff and obligations for managers designed to set out literally the way that ICL wanted to run its business. The seven commitments and the key messages they contained were:

1   *Commitment to change.* Success in our company now depends on each individual's willingness to accept change as something valuable, something to be welcomed, something to be responded to with energy and resourcefulness. Our business *is* change.

2   *Commitment to customers.* The overriding importance of the needs and expectations of our customers should condition all our thinking and govern all our planning. We are now a business driven by the business needs of our market.

3   *Commitment to excellence.* ICL's sights are now set on world success. That demands excellence in everything we undertake. And excellence will be achieved only by adopting 'can do' attitudes and the highest levels of co-operation and teamwork throughout the company.

4   *Commitment to teamwork.* Effective teamwork produces results far superior to anything the individuals could achieve working in isolation. To secure this $1 + 1 = 3$ return, our teamwork must be based on the need to heighten the capabilities, competence and contribution of each individual.

5   *Commitment to achievement.* ICL is an achievement company. Recognition, rewards, promotion and opportunities for career and job development depend absolutely on results delivered.

6   *Commitment to people development.* We are a people company. Our main strength lies in the quality and skill of the people who work here. Real progress will come about only by constantly developing and improving our skills. Development of this kind – people development – is one of the basic requirements for business success.

7   *Commitment to creating a productivity showcase. All* our systems, *all* aspects of our performance should be of 'showcase' standard – a standard which gives customers something to strive for.

It was greeted, as Don Beattie said, with a predictable mixture of support and cynisism, but it was the beginning of a completely new process. Although the words were carefully thought out and excellent in their own way, the symbolism of publishing such a document was probably more important than the detail of the words. But the set of seven commitments provided a backdrop – a reference and guide for activities within the company.

The educational programmes
In itself, of course, the 'ICL Way' was not going to do anything. At the same time, therefore, major educational programmes were commissioned. Entitled 'Core Management Development Programmes', the objective was to

communicate the strategic vision *and* the rationale behind it to all managers in ICL, and to reinforce the values of the 'ICL Way'.

Major shifts were needed in the way that people thought, made their decisions and conducted their lives in the company. Some of them can be summarized as follows:

FROM		TO
technology-led	→	marketing-led
tactical and short term	→	strategic, long term
internal focus	→	external focus
try and do everything	→	specialized target markets
parochial	→	company commitment
procedure-bound	→	innovative and open-minded
UK expert	→	global competitor

To put this programme into place ICL engaged two experts on strategic capability – C K Pralahad of the University of Michigan and Gary Hamel of the London Business School. They immersed themselves in ICL and its strategies and, together with internal resources, developed the most important programme, 'Developing strategic capability'.

The concept was to take major hierarchical levels in the organization and develop linked, appropriate events for each level. This was to be top-down training – mandatory for all, starting with the board.

At the same time ICL introduced a major marketing programme. Using Insead's MARKSTRAT model, and working with professors from Tulane University in the US, a six-part course in professional marketing covering a wide audience was instituted by ICL. This was to give direct support to the company's market strategies, by introducing the vital element of customer focus.

More recently ICL has commenced a third major cultural training programme for all employees, based on 'Quality as a way of life', again in support of the major business objective of becoming known for quality and reliability.

Thus the 'ICL Way' gave the company the basis of a shared vision for what we wanted to do. All these programmes were designed to give support for ICL's culture, objectives and strategies for tomorrow. They also brought home to all our managers the stark realization that ICL's human resources were a prime source of competitive advantage in its fight for market share.

The International Stock Exchange

Rhiannon Chapman described the International Stock Exchange as an organization in transition.

> We were a private civil service operating in a highly protected market. We were employed by the practitioners in that market to provide services and at the end of the day they wrote the

cheque to cover our costs. We weren't in the business of making profit. Well, we are now much more like other companies, not necessarily looking to make a profit but certainly to manage our own financial viability. We had to learn to see our member firms as customers and to market our services to them in a professional way. We have to be able to demonstrate the value of our markets and services: they are free to do their business elsewhere if we do not support them effectively.

Particularly in the build up to 'big bang' from 1983 onwards, we have been through a dramatic process of change. Over half our staff have joined us since 'big bang' in October 1986 and we have become a completely different organization because the skills we now have, and the skills we need to build on are quite different to those we were concerned with before.

So in this process of change, I was well pleased to be part of everything that was happening and in fact it fell to me because I was leading the corporate department for staff all the way through the changes. I was also best placed to set up the management conferencing activities we needed. At a very early stage in my time here I began to get people used to the idea that management conferences were things that would happen. They were not just 'talk, talk' but were actually workshops and problem-solving groups. So we built in from the outset, thinking about changes in the nature of the organization – how we needed to get where we are today, how we needed to get to the future.

These conferences were to do with skilling up the whole senior management group to gain an awareness of the issues confronting us and to plan how we were going to deal with these issues.

The MB Group

The MB Group's approach to cultural change was christened 'Creating a climate for change'. Key extracts from the paper written by Geoff Armstrong and Mike Kirkman are given below.

Mission statement

In the mission statement the group set itself ambitious strategic guidelines. We have declared that we will achieve worldwide leadership in our chosen fields by an emphasis on customer needs, technical excellence and manufacturing performance. Since the mission statement we have also set ourselves the target of doubling our sales by the early 1990s.

Such a mission requires managers to set ambitious stretching targets, with reference to the best international standards, to foster innovation and to be truly strategic in their planning. The mission will be achieved only if managers at all levels are driven by continuous dissatisfaction with current performance so that the group constantly strives to do better and if an environment is created which generates willing contribution from employees at all levels.

While much has been achieved, there is a widespread recognition that the pace of change needs to accelerate. This paper sets out the plan for a campaign for change, based on:

- a shared agenda against which progress can be measured;

- a communications programme aimed at internal and external audiences;

- an increased investment in training so that managers develop both the skills and the vision to manage the change process.

Elements of the campaign
The proposed campaign consists of three main elements:

1 *The agenda for change.* There is a need for an agenda which inlists general support.

The chairman, the chief executive and other executive group directors will visit each of the managing directors and their boards on their own territory, in order to 'review progress in meeting the chairman's key tasks, especially those relating to achievement of a change environment'.

These meetings will be structured so as to:

- recognize and reinforce achievements to date;

- bring out the interdependence of all Metal Box businesses and the benefits to be gained by all of them from the improved performance and reputation of each part of the group;

- encourage managers to draw out the contribution of employees at all levels and then to give recognition to their achievements;

- seek managers' support for, or alterations to, the agenda for change;

- seek comments on the areas identified on the agenda as they relate to each business;

- elicit discussion on areas where managers feel they and their staff need help and/or training;

- stimulate discussion on the company's overall objectives and on how the divisional boards will pursue the debate with their own management teams;

- secure managers' commitment to develop explicit plans against their priority change objectives.

Key issues
In accelerating the pace of change the following are key issues:

- the need for an explicit agenda;

- the description of the desired behaviour so that the agenda is more than a collection of 'buzz words';

- ways of setting agreed objectives and of measuring performance and progress towards them, both short and long term;

- an environment of support in which recognition of achievement to date will reinforce confidence to do more;

- executive group leadership which encourages managers to be bold and innovative and to harness the ideas and talents of all employees in the search for better ways of doing things;

- collaboration and partnership between business and corporate resources;

- the generation of a widespread attitude among all employees that encourages change and innovation.

The campaign
It is proposed to run a campaign across Metal Box for a broad programme of change, rather than to tackle each change objective as a separate initiative or in a piecemeal way. External experience, increasingly reported by industrialists, consultants and academics, leads strongly to the view that the bolder and more visionary the agenda set by top management, the more effective and faster are the results achieved. If employees at all levels can be convinced that radical change is being adopted across the range of the company's activities and is directed towards major improvements in overall performance (and thereby to continued investment and greater job security and satisfaction), they are more likely to support a 'hearts and minds' campaign and change their own behaviour.

The proposed campaign will require a sustained effort by executive group members and by business and functional managers over at least a two- to three-year period to establish the climate of innovation, creative risk-taking and performance optimization we are seeking as the recognizable Metal Box culture.

Although heavy use will be made of experience gained by other companies in their programmes of change (and we will draw on their consultants where relevant), there is unlikely to be any single company we can take as a model for the actions appropriate to us. The campaign will therefore need to be run as a visible, high-commitment crusade to establish values and action styles which we believe will lead to more effective performance and future competitiveness. It will be that commitment, rather than unequivocally demonstrable results in the early stages, that forms the base and the motivation for our sustained, urgently-driven programme of change.

2   *Communications.* In parallel with the 'agenda for change' initiatives to be taken by the business units and functions, which though management-led and individually tailored are all aimed at common objectives, there will also be a corporate level programme driven by the chairman and executive group, aimed at internal and, later, external audiences.

Internally the aims of the programme will be to:

- restate the commitment of Metal Box to be an excellent company, in particular to be better than its competitors in meeting and exceeding the needs and expectations of its customers;

- explain why it is important for Metal Box to gain and keep competitive edge by tailoring everything it does to serving customers better than anyone else (e.g. flexibility, lead times, quality, design innovation, cost performance, original thinking, ingenuity);

- describe the sorts of behaviour appropriate to success illustrated plentifully by examples of best practice;

- provide support, recognition and public acknowledgement of employees at all levels who take initiatives to advance competitive edge;

- motivate employees to give their best because they are proud to work for Metal Box and because they believe that the improvements sought are worthy of their committed support.

3 *Training*. We will increase our investment in training so that, building on the work that has already been done, all managers will have the opportunity to update their strategic skills and to share the corporate values underlying this programme for change. With the help of outside consultants and top-level academics we will run pilot courses designed to assist managers to implement the agenda for change; we will arrange training to meet specific management skill requirements identified as a common priority (e.g. marketing) during the review meetings; and we will increase the use of the major UK, European and American business programmes so as to maximize the personal development and individual contribution of managers.

Rumbelows

Culture change at Rumbelows was characterized by STAR (Sales Transformation at Rumbelows), an ambitious programme for retraining the entire retail workforce of over 2,000 in just three months. The programme emerged from an assessment that the market was dominated by a number of national chains and big discount houses, thus revealing a marketing opportunity. As Jeff Roberts said:

> There was no major player providing a service to people who were less confident about what they wanted to buy but nevertheless were sensitive to quality and service.

Having identified this market sector, the company brought in design consultants to give its 430 shops a softer, more up-market look. Changing the visual image of the shops was not enough, however. The past three years have also seen major changes in the company's organizational structure.

> What we've tried to do over the past few years is basically change the culture of the whole business in terms of its management style.

Until recently, the company was run along traditional hierarchical lines. A less formal and more open approach was introduced with fewer people on the board in a bid to decentralize decision-making. Changes were also made in the previously top-heavy management structure, with the removal of a whole management level.

The next step was to take a look at the business and its corporate aims. Consultants brought in for this purpose discovered that the company's operational effectiveness was the easiest thing to improve in the short term. Jeff Roberts explains:

> As a result of studies in the field we found that because the business had been through this major change ... we didn't actually have a cohesive shop management process.

Representatives from personnel management, field management and sales formed a working party. With the help of consultants they drew up suggestions for improving operational effectiveness and introduced the STAR programme for implementing these proposals.

The entire retail workforce was retrained through STAR between June and September 1988. Branch and regional managers went on a course of two one-week modules covering shop management, people management, the newly defined sales procedures, the role of the shop manager and selling skills. The programme ended with a reorientation session for the new regional managers, with each division taking half a day to present its function.

References

1   BECKHARD, Richard. *Organization development: strategy and models.* Reading, Mass., Addison-Wesley, 1969
2   KANTER, Rosabeth Moss. *The change masters.* London, Allen & Unwin, 1984
3   SCHEIN, E. H. 'Coming to a new awareness of corporate culture'. *Sloan Management Revue.* Winter, 1984
4   DEAL, T. E. *and* KENNEDY, A. *Corporate cultures.* Reading, Mass. Addison-Wesley, 1982

10 Organization Planning and the Bottom Line

ORGANIZATION PLANNING AIMS

Organization planning aims to provide an environment in which people can direct their efforts as individuals and teams to the achievement of the organization's objectives for growth and profitability. It endeavours to structure organizations which:

- are fit for their purpose;
- have a lean and hungry look about them;
- use people's talents effectively;
- are flexible enough to respond to change but still provide a framework which helps people to understand how they are expected to make their contribution to improving bottom-line performance;
- while differentiating activities and operating close to distinctive markets, provide for integrated effort;
- encourage individual enterprise and endeavour without prejudicing teamwork.

Achieving all these aims, which can easily conflict, is not an easy task. Essentially they are all about planning how best to deploy and utilize human resources profitably, a responsibility which can firmly and properly be placed within the remit of the personnel function.

John Hougham notes that:

> Clearly part of the process of becoming efficient is down-sizing, taking structure out where it doesn't pay for itself, and finding ways of breaking down the chimneys in the organization – manufacturing chimneys, product development chimneys, whatever.

He has no doubt that in these circumstances:

> Organization planning is very much part of the personnel function at Ford. We've probably got the longest experience in

130

Britain of actually running an integrated European operation –
100,000 people. Now the organization structure that supports
all this is a very sophisticated and complex beast and keeping it
tuned up is clearly a personnel responsibility.

Organization planning is not just about structuring and restructuring
organizations – regrouping activities, eliminating layers of management,
decentralizing or divisionalizing, or achieving better integration across
departmental boundaries. It is also about resourcing the changing structure
with the right people and making sure that they know what they are doing
and are equipped with the competences to do it.

John Hougham, again, on how organization planning and resourcing in
the broadest sense are linked together:

Historically we had plants with five or six thousand people,
controlled by a plant manager and with a chimney organization –
manufacturing, engineering, maintenance, quality control and
so on. We started some years ago to convert that structure into
an area management structure. We did it first of all at the senior
management level. A manager, instead of being just a
production manager would become a general manager, with all
the resources he required to run his bit of the business. We have
extended that downwards through the organization to every
performance level, converting production foremen to area
foremen with all the resources they require to do the job.

Now you need much broader, better qualified people to do
that job. It's a more responsible job because they no longer have
any alibis. They can't blame someone else, and say 'I'm sorry,
the machine has broken down,' because they have now got all
the resources to deal with it themselves. So it's a more interesting
job.

But the concerns, and these come back to the personnel
function, are first, developing that organization and, secondly,
resourcing it, because many of the people had to be converted
into a quite different manager or supervisor from what they had
been over the past 25 years. The intention was that they should
become mini general managers and that was a massive selection
and training job.

ORGANIZATION PLANNING – PROBLEMS AND OPPORTUNITIES

Sometime ago, Burns and Stalker made a fundamental point:

The beginning of administrative wisdom is the awareness that
there is no one optimum type of management system[1]

There is no ideal form of organization structure, there are no hard and fast rules about organization design. Everything is contingent on the situation and, as Chandler says, 'structure follows strategy'.[2]

In other words, the purpose and strategy of the organization as well as its environment and technology will determine its structure. And its methods of operation, its organizational processes, will be strongly influenced by its culture. In addition there is the fact that, whatever the organization theory purists may say, organizations have, to a degree, to be structured around people; they may have to be modified, especially at senior levels, to fit the particular strengths and, sometimes, weaknesses of job holders.

This sound like a problem but, in fact, it provides an opportunity. A flexible approach to structuring and staffing the organization can be adopted. It will be recognized that the dangers of slavishly following the 'organization-reorganization-disorganization' route can be avoided if care is taken to build jobs around people's strengths and competences, as long as those match the short- and long-term needs of the organization. This is where the personnel function can exert considerable influence on the organization planning process by analyzing and identifying the competences required, finding and developing the right people and designing jobs in a way which will help them to maximize their contribution to the bottom line.

The rise of the flexible, responsive and global firm as mentioned in Chapter 1 can also present organizational problems. These may be compounded by new technology, especially information technology. The questions raised at the end of that chapter on how to create unified vision in an organization of specialists, how to devise a structure for an organization of task forces, how to provide careers in the flatter organization, and how to get people to accept operational flexibility as a way of life, all need answering. And there are no easy answers.

Rosabeth Moss Kanter comments that:

> Managers and professionals function in a world that often contains vague assignments, overlapping territories, uncertain authority and resources, and the mandate to work through teams rather than unilaterally.[3]

She goes on to say:

> Innovating companies provide the freedom to act, which arouses the desire to act ... and some kinds of uncertainty create opportunities.

The opportunity for the personnel function in these circumstances is to help in the development of an environment in which the virtues of enforced collaboration are recognized and people learn to live in intersecting territories and accept that multi-disciplinary problems can best be solved by project teams. At Book Club Associates the project team approach was built into the culture at a very early stage in its history and has successfully achieved inter-departmental co-operation in such areas as developing new products or solving company-wide problems. It is accepted that these teams have a distinct role which need not interfere with the day-to-day managerial process. And, incidentally, it was the personnel director who had the overall responsibility for seeing that these teams functioned effectively.

Getting people to live happily in the flexible firm is a matter first of selecting and promoting people who can cope with, in fact thrive on, ambiguity and, secondly, of working on the culture of the organization to develop commitment to values which emphasize the importance of flexibility and teamwork. Career plans can be developed which do not limit people to ascending the rungs of much truncated managerial ladders. Instead, they can demonstrably provide opportunities for professional and technical staff to grow within their specialism as the organization grows.

Another problem for anyone involved in organization planning is that there no longer seem to be any rules to the game. True, decentralization and flatter organizations are seen as good things, but in every other aspect, anything goes. Peter Reay feels this:

> I sometimes wish I had a stronger tool kit in this field. The behavioural bases that one has used in the past are fine up to a point, and all the mechanical, organization design things about how many people should report to a boss and so on, are quite useful from a common sense point of view. But I feel the lack of a basic discipline or methodology.

Again, a problem but also an opportunity. Organization planning is no longer simply a matter of drawing lines on a chart and putting names in boxes. Neither is it writing endless job descriptions. As Peter Wickens said:

> This is a management institution which I think leads to inflexibility rather than flexibility. So we have no job descriptions, no grade levels – totally generic job titles. If you're an engineer you're an engineer. You don't need a job description, you just get on and do the job you're paid to do.

Organization planning still involves designing structures, albeit flexible ones. But it is now much more about defining purpose and outputs and providing for their accomplishment by developing and encouraging organizational processes which promote effective interaction, teamwork and commitment. The emphasis is not so much on who does what as on what results have to be achieved and the best ways of working together to attain them. This is where organization planning merges with organization development.

ORGANIZATION DEVELOPMENT AND THE BOTTOM LINE

Organization development, or OD, has become somewhat discredited in recent years as the creature of the behavioural scientists. Academics and management consultants who used to preach its virtues now talk about culture change. In some cases it is only the name that has changed, and culture change practitioners are still really living in their behavioural science past.

But there is a difference. Culture change programmes are geared to achieving fundamental changes to the norms, values and behaviours in an organization in order to produce specific and quantifiable improvements in company performance. OD programmes were more concerned with organizational processes such as interaction, co-operation, involvement, planning and conflict, almost, it sometimes seemed, as ends in themselves.

In practice, the distinction is not all that significant. A culture change programme must be concerned with organizational processes such as those mentioned above, although it may place much greater emphasis on leadership and performance (the lunatic fringe of the OD movement seemed to think that the only purpose of an organization was to create one big happy family). And even such a dedicated OD specialist as Richard Beckhard could put the following characteristic as the first of those defining a healthy organization:

> The total organization, the significant sub-parts, and individuals manage their work against goals and plans for the achievement of these goals.[4]

ORGANIZATION PROCESSES

Organization planning and development should concentrate on these key processes:

1 *Leadership* – how it is exercised throughout the organization. Vision and the determination to turn that vision into reality are essential characteristics at the top. But this must be converted into inspirational leadership, and at each level there must be people who are capable of passing on the message and inspiring their staff to follow their example.

2 *Teamwork* – how to develop cohesive and productive teams within departments and, more importantly, across the organization. The flexible firm has to eliminate rigid boundaries.

3 *Interaction* – getting individuals to work together effectively on a one-to-one basis or within teams.

4 *Communication* – ensuring that the communications flows within the organization not only keep everyone well informed on what they need

to know but also create a sense of belonging and develop commitment to the organization and its values.

Organization designers too often concentrate on the formal organization, virtually ignoring the informal processes that actually get the work done. Organization developers appreciate that attention must be given to these processes while recognizing that structure is still necessary as a framework for action.

References

1 BURNS, T, *and* STALKER, G. M. *The management of innovation.* London, Tavistock Publications, 1961
2 CHANDLER, A. *Strategy and structure: chapters in the history of American industrial enterprise.* Cambridge, Mass., MIT Press, 1962
3 KANTER, Rosabeth Moss. *The change masters.* New York, Simon & Schuster, 1983
4 BECKHARD, Richard. *Organization development: strategy and models.* Reading, Mass., Addison-Wesley, 1969

11 Competitive Resourcing

WHY RESOURCING IS A COMPETITIVE BUSINESS

Leading-edge companies seek competitive advantage and added value in order to maximize their long-term growth and profitability. They can only succeed in doing this if they ensure that a flow of talented people enters and progresses through their organizations. Resourcing is a competitive business. High-quality staff are in short supply. They have to be attracted to join and motivated to stay with the company. As Barry Curnow says:

> The scarce resource, which is the people resource, really is the one that makes the difference at the margin, that makes one firm competitive over another and vice versa.

A competitive approach to resourcing is necessary not only because of a shortage of talent, which will be exacerbated by the demographic problems of the 1990s, but also because of the need to obtain and develop entrepreneurial managers who will make the business grow and add significantly to the bottom line.

Competitive resourcing is a strategic process. It starts by defining the sort of business the company is in and where it is going. It then decides what the company wants in the way of human resources to reach its objectives and how the people it needs are to be recruited, trained and developed.

COMPETITIVE RESOURCING STRATEGY

As Tony Vineall remarked:

> Getting hold of the talent, sustaining the talent, and giving it career space to develop, have of their own right become prime responsibilities of the personnel function.

136

To fulfil these responsibilities the aims of a resourcing strategy should be to:

1 Devise an organization-wide selection, development and career management system that supports the business strategy;
2 Create internal flows of people that match the business strategy;
3 Mesh strategic planning with executive skills.

Achieving the aims

To achieve these aims it is necessary to:

(a) develop a corporate culture, climate and management style which will enable the company to compete for the right sort of people and help to commit them to the organization;

(b) ensure that human resource plans are integrated with the business plans and provide clear guidance on the necessary recruitment, training, management development and career management policies and programmes;

(c) provide for organization plans to be prepared and put into effect which help the business to make the best use of its human resources;

(d) following the overall human resource and organization planning processes, identify the competences required in each area and at each level, ensuring that they match the particular needs of the organization;

(e) plan and implement performance-related training programmes which are designed to impact, directly or indirectly, on the bottom line;

(f) plan and implement management development and career management programmes aimed at providing the future flows of managerial talent required by the organization.

CORPORATE CULTURE DEVELOPMENT

Barry Curnow believes that:

> Employers are having to compete for scarce skills and they're having to compete on whether or not they are attractive. It's no longer pay that gives one company a competitive edge over another in attracting people in this scarcity situation. It's actually whether the managers, the professionals, the young people, believe that they want to buy into the values, plans, philosophy and mission of that company. . . .
> What you have to do is to make your company more attractive than the company down the road to a prospective candidate.

This means that climate and culture and management style and leadership become very powerful attractors and motivators of scarce people.

Don Beattie makes the same point, although somewhat differently:

The guy with 10 years' experience in the IT industry, walks on water, what is going to make him join STC as opposed to any of the other players in the market? And it's not going to be that you've got a smarter compensation package than anyone else. It's going to be something about the sort of company it is, as exuded by its 'corporate image', as exuded by the way its managers behave, by the sort of reputation it has built up.

Cultural change programmes, as described in Chapter 9, are therefore prime contributors to successful competitive resourcing.

HUMAN RESOURCE PLANNING AND THE BOTTOM LINE

Human resource plans impact directly on the bottom line, first because they indicate clearly what sort of people and how many people are needed to implement the business plan and, secondly, because if they contribute to the retention of staff – cutting back wastage – they can significantly reduce recruitment, training and induction costs.

Human resource planning is something that *must* go hand in hand with business planning. It is fatal to the future prosperity of the company if it becomes no more than a piece of arithmetic added on almost as an after-thought. It should be related to market forecasts, manufacturing plans, perceptions about new products, programmes for introducing new technology, financial constraints and organization plans.

The information available to prepare the human resource plan often contains many judgements and much subjectivity. Admittedly, if there is a good personnel database, human resource planning models can and should be developed to forecast future flows in relation to various assumptions about business trends. At Book Club Associates a planning model is used in the distribution division which is linked to various business and financial models and, in relation to alternative parameters, forecasts precise staffing requirements over the next two years.

Such models can be used to answer 'what if' questions at the business planning stage. If there are going to be shortfalls, they can indicate needs to train, to retrain, to achieve greater flexibility in the use of people or to increase mechanization, if it is profitable to do so.

Mike Stanton deplores the fact that 'most organizations operate on the principle that people can be found, somehow; fundamentally a wrong assumption, but that's the way they work.' He suggests that businesses should be continually asking the question:

> What sort of workforce will the organization need to deliver its future? For example, it doesn't matter whether a business is going to expand or contract or remain in a steady state. All of these scenarios may result in problems concerning people management. If it's going to expand, it will want managers who can take on bigger jobs and employees who are willing to be mobile so that thay can move to where the operation is going to grow. If it's going to contract, it needs employees who will accept the contraction, accept redeployment, work flexibly. If it's going to stay in a steady state it needs a workforce that will not become demotivated by the fact that it's not growing.

Human resource planning embraces acquisition plans, redeployment plans, training and retraining plans, management development plans and, importantly, because of the direct savings involved, retention plans. Len Peach emphasises the significance of the latter:

> Strategically it is important to make sure that the right manpower is there in the 1990s. It is important for the bottom line, especially when training costs keep on going up. IBM's labour turnover over the last five years averaged about two and a half per cent. Now that's important, because IBM's training costs are very significant against a background where its imployees are highly marketable.

Referring to the attitude survey conducted by IBM every two years Len Peach said that:

> Everyone is surveyed. The survey is then presented both to top management and to the group that completed the survey by the immediate manager. Next, a plan is put together to try to rectify any problems which actually appear. That really is the essence of retention, bringing out problems both individually and collectively and taking action to make sure that they don't develop to a point where they are registered in the form of significant losses . . . losses which can clearly be seen as major in terms of the bottom line or as assets to the company.

Retention planning involves an analysis of the causes of wastage through attitude surveys and leaving interviews and, as appropriate, action in one or more of the following areas:

- respecifying requirements to make sure that the right skills are being sought – neither over- nor under-skilling;

- tightening up recruitment procedures to ensure that candidates and new starters meet the specification;

- ensuring that salary levels are competitive, not only to recruit but also to retain;

- operating an equitable salary system which rewards people according to performance and motivates rather than demotivates (some salary systems are better at the latter);

- influencing and shaping the corporate culture as defined by climate and management style to make people believe that the organization is worth working for;

- increasing commitment by ensuring that everyone believes in the organization's mission and values and that people see the benefit to themselves as well as to the organization in pursuing their careers with the company;

- improving induction arrangements so that new employees quickly settle down into their jobs;

- making training more effective in equipping people with the skills they need to do their jobs and to get satisfaction out of doing them well;

- providing career ladders which clearly indicate how people can progress in the organization, what they must do to achieve promotion and how the company will help them;

- through the performance review system, providing counselling to employees who are doubtful about the future and whom the company wishes to retain;

- training managers and supervisors on how they can improve retention rates, and in leadership and counselling skills.

The impact of demographics

Clearly, demographic trends into the 1990s are or should be a major cause of concern for all organizations. Alan Fell comments that while corporate planners attempt to look at the future on a macro level, the human resource planner has to consider trends on a micro basis. Questions have to be asked concerning demographics such as:

> What does that mean for the corporation at micro level? What does it mean for the trading business? You have to focus on the right questions, because, never mind the broad brush stuff, when you get down to it, many firms are not large employers of school leavers. But there's this terrible problem: 16-year-olds have a habit of becoming 23-year-olds. No one's quite worked out how to stop it. They could have a demographic problem in five years' time.

Len Peach explains how the demographic situation in the 1990s is affecting the National Health Service and how a retention strategy impacts on the bottom line:

> Because of demographic changes in the normal recruitment population for nursing, the NHS will be faced with significant changes in the labour market. The result will be that it won't be able to recruit the same numbers from that segment. It takes 25 per cent of that female group. To meet its needs, the NHS would have in the 1990s to recruit 40 per cent of the group. Well, that looks impossible, recognizing that this is the same group that supplies the banks and the insurance companies with much of their senior clerical staff. So the NHS has to have a strategy on how it is going to recruit in the 1990s. Not only on how it is going to recruit in terms of widening the catchment area, but also on how it is going to retain staff.
>
> Thus the nurse's clinical grading structure is concerned with the 1990s, not today. It is concerned with making sure that the NHS offers the career progression which will provide the professional nurse with an attraction to stay within it rather than going outside.
>
> If the NHS could save one per cent on labour turnover, it would save 3,000 trained nurses, each costing £30,000 to train. And that goes straight to the bottom line and makes more money available for patient care.

Questions to be answered

The human resource planning process should provide answers to the following questions:

1 What are the implications of the business plan on our human resource requirements?

2 What have we got now in the way of human resources?

3 What, on the basis of reasonable assumptions, are we likely to have during each of the years of the business plan?

4 What deficits or surpluses are likely to develop over the period of the business plan?

5 What actions are we going to take to deal with deficits or surpluses, e.g.

   - recruitment
   - redeployment
   - retraining
   - multi-skilling

- management development
- succession planning
- retention planning
- selective recruitment freezes
- redundancy.

IDENTIFYING COMPETENCES

Competences describe what people must do to reach a satisfactory level of performance in a particular job. There are said to be certain universal competences such as communication and leadership skills which are common to all management jobs. But each organization and each job within that organization will have specific requirements which need to be identified for recruiting, training and career development purposes.

Corporate requirements

As Chandler remarked in his classic study of American industrial enterprise, 'structure follows strategy'.[1] What the organization is and sets out to do not only determines its organization structure but also the type of people, especially managers, it wants. Key executives need to be matched to the business strategy and General Electric classifies its general managers in accordance with the well-known Boston Consulting Group's portfolio matrix:

Business type	*General manager requirement*
• wildcat	• grower
• star	• defender
• cash cow	• caretaker
• dog	• undertaker

A study of the General Electric portfolio might indicate, for example, that there is a shortage of growers for the wildcats and too many undertakers in growth areas. Appropriate resourcing action can then be taken.

Texas Instruments believes that it is necessary to match management style to product life cycle. As a product moves through different phases of its life cycle, different levels of management skills become dominant. It could be disastrous, for instance, to put risk-taking entrepreneurs in charge of mature cash cow businesses. It could be equally disastrous to put cost-cutting efficiency orientated managers in charge of growing businesses where they might stifle initiative and prevent the business gaining market share.

A definition of the competences required in a start-up situation may state that the major job thrusts are to:

- create a vision of the business;
- establish core technical and marketing expertise;
- build the management team.

The characteristics required for candidates for such a position might be:

- a clear view of the finished business;
- hands-on orientation, i.e. a 'do-er';
- skill in devising entry strategies and launching products;
- in-depth knowledge of critical technical areas;
- broad knowledge of key business functions;
- high-level energy and stamina;
- organizing ability;
- team-building capabilities;
- staffing skills;
- personal magnetism and charisma.

Managerial competences

Within the strategic framework which influences the competences required at general management level, it is possible to develop lists of the competences relevant for particular organizations. These can be used as criteria in assessment or development centres or a standard selection procedure.

For example, an international group in the finance sector describes its effective performers as:

- achievement orientated – they are strongly motivated by achievement, recognition and reward and possess an internal drive that continually urges them forward to higher levels;
- having a positive outlook – they are energetic, enthusiastic and want to make a unique personal contribution to every job they do;
- being reliable – they are noted for always doing a job properly with attention to relevant detail;
- being adaptable – they are flexible, self-organized and self-monitoring;
- being able to organize themselves and those around them to meet targets effectively and on time;

- having a natural affinity for people, well-developed leadership skills, and a high degree of maturity in dealing with others;

- understanding that their progress can be enhanced by building up the performance of their teams – they are therefore keen to advance the interests of others as well as themselves;

- good communicators, both face to face and on paper.

In W H Smith, the performance areas used in its general management assessment centre are:

1 *Self management:* ability to organize, plan and manage time;

2 *Interaction management and leadership:* ability to work constructively with peers and seniors and to interface with other functions;

3 *Financial management:* financial knowledge and ability to make sound financial judgements;

4 *Marketing management:* ability to consider and appraise strategic marketing issues, recognizing and responding to strengths and opportunities;

5 *Strategic planning:* ability to think and act at a strategic level and to define clear longer range business-related objectives;

6 *Situation assessment:* ability to make an analysis of a business situation, to identify its key variables and to generate appropriate objectives and courses of action;

7 *Staff management:* ability to work successfully with subordinates and/or experts to obtain information and understanding of unfamiliar subjects;

8 *Manpower planning:* ability to determine future requirements against available resources, identifying training and development needs;

9 *Oral communications:* ability to speak clearly and present or argue a situation in a logical and positive manner which gains commitment and support;

10 *Written communications:* ability to create business-like correspondence and, where appropriate, present well-argued proposals supported by relevant data.

Individual job competences

Individual job competences can be defined by the normal processes of job and skills analysis. There are many ways of doing this, as described in the textbooks, but an interesting variation was developed at Book Club Associates in association with the Hay system of job evaluation.

This involved taking a job hierarchy, for example, copywriters in the creative department, and preparing job statements for each level which listed the principal accountabilities. The job evaluation indicated the level of each job in relation to the three Hay factors of know-how, accountability, and problem solving. The job profile enlarged these definitions as necessary to establish 'competency criteria' – what job holders needed to know and be able to do at each level. These defined entry qualifications on recruitment or promotion for each grade in terms of knowledge, skills and ability to perform specified tasks. A career progression curve, as shown in Figure 11.1, could then be drawn which related Hay points to salaries for each job and referred to the competency criteria.

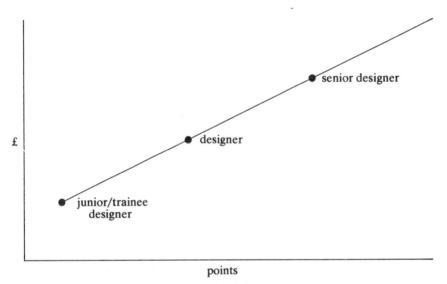

points

Figure 11.1 Career progression curve

This approach enabled the creative department to resource itself with people who had relevant skills and experience. Careers could be planned, as could salary progression. For the individuals concerned, the system provided them with guidance on what they needed to be able to do to be promoted. It showed them not only how their career could progress but also how their salary could progress with it.

HUMAN RESOURCE DEVELOPMENT AND THE BOTTOM LINE

Performance related training

Performance related training is designed to develop competences which impact directly on the bottom line. It involves relating training specifically to performance requirements – for example, those following the introduction of a new product or system.

Terry Murphy explains how it was done at Abbey National:

> Every time we designed or developed a new product we would involve a trainer in the development team. So, as the product was developed, the training was developed. Before the product was actually launched there was a training package designed for the branches so that each branch could start to train its staff in all aspects of the product before it was launched.
>
> We then extended this into the systems area, so that every time we developed a new computer system, a new investment system or a new mortgage system we involved the trainer in the systems development. The benefits of this were twofold: one was that the trainers learned a lot more about the systems we were launching and, two, the systems designers learned a lot about how these systems had to be put over to the users, and more still about user friendliness, etc. It pulled trainers into the fabric of the business and also pulled specialists into the fabric of the presentation of the new product, system or procedure.

Lynn Richards also sees training as only being worthwhile if it makes a positive impact on the business:

> We only train on the basis of what impact we can see happening as a result of it. We don't just do it in an airy-fairy 'Well we need to do some developmental training to improve people's performance' sense. We do product related training and we can actually see what contribution that training is making to the bottom line. We measure. If we do some training on, say, welding equipment, we look at the improvement in the contribution from that product area as a result of that activity.

The W H Smith approach to performance related training

W H Smith developed its performance related training policy for managers following a systematic review of management training. Managers said they enjoyed attending courses and the level of nominations was rising. However, there was no proof that they were gaining any practical benefit from the courses or that W H Smith's investment of nearly £1m. in 1985 was justified.

W H Smith was also aware that it was ignoring some important techniques which could make management training more effective in the workplace. As a result, it started to look for an approach to management training which would 'measurably improve job performance'. This meant making sure that managers understood and could implement the systems and procedures to ensure consistency throughout a geographically dispersed organization. It also meant leaving aside the universal theories of management in favour of much closer attention to the different detailed routines which apply in the various businesses within the W H Smith group.

In W H Smith's search for this new approach it found many of the components it was seeking in such areas as skills training, student centred learning and assessment centre methodology. In the latter case, the extensive use of assessment centres for all levels of management established that the analysis of behaviour during the programme was a valuable way of identifying development needs as well as establishing promotability.

W H Smith did not, however, find these components assembled together coherently and applied to management training. As a result, they designed the approach they now call 'performance related training' (PRT). the purpose of PRT is to identify individual training needs and provide relevant and effective training to meet them.

An important part of the PRT process is the profiling of key skills. The newly appointed manager undertakes exercises in the key skills of the job to which he or she has been promoted. His or her performance is compared with the standard expected of an experienced manager in the same position. A below-standard performance indicates a training need which is met by the most suitable of a variety of different responses. These include residential courses, guided study, assignments or individual coaching. Following training, managers undertake a further exercise to confirm that their performance is now of the required standard.

W H Smith believes that performance related training has enabled it to confirm the practical benefits of management training in measurable terms. It anchors management training firmly to the needs of the current job and ensures that managers have the competences and skills to carry out all the functions of the jobs for which they are being paid.

Ten ways in which performance related training *can* contribute to the bottom line

Performance related training:

1   Makes sure that the company's mission statement is not only seen and heard by employees but is also understood, accepted and acted upon.

2   Communicates and gains commitment to the values of the organization – for example, those concerned with total quality improvement or customer care.

3   Is a most effective instrument for achieving cultural change.

4   Channels attitudes and beliefs in appropriate directions – for example, to become more entrepreneurial, to be more aware of the impact of specific behaviours on the bottom line.

5   Assists organizational change by equipping people with the new skills required.

6   Promotes flexibility by helping people to acquire new skills (multi-skilling).

7   Supports innovation and growth by making sure that people are capable of implementing change and carrying out new tasks.

8   Speeds up the induction of trainees, starters and newly promoted employees, bringing them quickly to the experienced and effective worker's standard of performance.

9   Provides and develops the talent specified by the company's strategic plan to achieve longer-term growth and profitability targets.

10 Improves organizational performance generally by filling the gaps between what people can do and what they should be able to do.

Ten ways in which to ensure that performance related training *does* contribute to the bottom line

1   Develop a training strategy which is integrated with and supports the business strategy.

2   Understand that innovation and change always generate training needs and cannot be made fully effective unless those training needs are satisfied.

3   Analyze the opportunities and threats facing the organization to identify areas where training could develop opportunities or could help to minimize the impact of threats.

4   Analyze the culture of the organization to identify areas where training could help to influence cultural changes.

5   Analyze organizational performance to identify failures or weaknesses that training might help to avoid in the future.

6   Assess human resource plans and analyze proposed organizational changes to determine the skills that are likely to be required in the future and the training implications of developing new skills.

7   Assess the training implications of increasing flexibility in such areas as multi-skilling.

8   Identify individual training and development needs through performance appraisal, assessment centres and analysis of the degree to which the competences required are possessed by individual job holders.

9   Ensure that managers and supervisors are fully aware of their training responsibilities and are equipped with the skills to fulfil them properly.

10 Seize every training opportunity as a chance to make a positive impact on the bottom line.

MANAGEMENT DEVELOPMENT AND THE BOTTOM LINE

Management development programmes aim to provide men and women of promise with a sequence of planned experience and training that will equip them for whatever level of responsibility they have the ability to reach. The assumptions are made that managers learn by doing and that the best form of development is self-development.

The organization helps this process by providing conditions conducive to faster growth and by instituting appraisal (including self-appraisal) and counselling processes which help individuals to develop their careers under the guidance of their managers and with whatever help the organization can provide. This will include formal training within and outside the company, but it will still be recognized that the principal method by which managers can be developed is by ensuring that they have the right variety of experience, in good time, in the course of their career. This experience can and should be supplemented, but never replaced, by courses carefully tuned and designed to meet particular needs. But the best training, which can be defined as the modification of behaviour through experience, will happen in the 'real' situation, i.e. in the normal course of work through coaching, projects and guided self-analysis and development.

Although the concept of a 'career' looms large in management development programmes, they do not exist simply to satisfy the aspirations of individual managers. Their principal purpose is to meet the organization's needs to provide for management succession and to ensure that it has managers equipped in specific ways to meet its objectives. The impact of management development activities on the bottom line is greatest when they are dedicated to growing entrepreneurial, profit-conscious managers, who are flexible, can cope with change and ambiguity, can take command, are commited to achievement, yet are considerate and caring in their dealings with their staff and colleagues.

Approaches to management development

The personnel function has a key part to play in management development. As Peter Hobbs says:

> I think that the principal contribution that personnel can make is about the development of people and the development of potential. The personnel role is really to say: 'Hey, this is a change in our working environment and we have got to respond to that, and how are people thinking about that?'

The contribution is not simply about administering the system of competency analysis, performance appraisals, potential reviews, succession plans and development programmes, although all these are important. It is much more about ensuring that managers at all levels are aware of their personal responsibility for developing their staff with the help of the processes supplied by the personnel department. So, as Terry Murphy put it, there has to be some discipline and there has to be a follow-up system.

> Part of the implied contract of people being appraised was that if a development need were identified it must be fulfilled – not it should, it must. So after the appraisals, the manpower development managers sat down with each general manager in turn, went through the development needs that came out of the appraisals and established a set of agreed methodologies for meeting those needs: sometimes training, sometimes coaching, sometimes secondment, sometimes a permanent move. We may send them away, we may do it in-house. But what we did insist on was that any training would be done in a prestigious way. In other words, we wouldn't carp about sending someone to Harvard if that was the right approach to meet his or her needs, and we would have the resources available to do that.
>
> Then we put in management audit disciplines and succession plans. First we audited our resources, secondly we prepared a succession plan which was based on an assessment of potential and thirdly, we followed these up with what we called a CAP, which was a career appraisal programme. . . .

Management development and career planning is a hands-on process which involves all levels of management. Members of the personnel function are there to persuade and to provide back up, which includes defining policies and managing processes as in the following examples.

Management development at Cadbury Schweppes

The personnel function at Cadbury Schweppes defined the group's management development policy by reference to the sort of manager it wants:

As a fast-growth company we need:

- ability moving up, pushing our top people
- managers in the top two to three levels with an international perspective
- managers who are information technology literate
- managers with capacities greater than their current job requires
- managers with commercial awareness but a human face
- a mix of managers who can:
  - integrate acquisitions
  - manage and organize growth
  - manage a maintenance environment

- a mix of managers with dominant skills for jobs requiring:
  - hands-on management, or
  - high-order integration skills, or
  - ideas-dominated leadership as the key for success.

The supporting recommendations to this policy were defined as being:

To undertake management development activities selectively and with clear focus. Priority should be given to activities with a big pay back. We will develop our top people who will pull the remaining up to new levels. To this end we should:

- Undertake a regular disciplined assessment of high-potential talent on an international basis.

- Adopt a common language for management development, building upon the model of leadership excellence and competency dimensions.

- Expand the general management training scheme on an international basis and have a small cadre from universities throughout the world who have planned careers.

- Have selective, planned job rotation across streams, countries and functions.

- Have a simple, flexible way for identifying and providing talent across streams.

- Continue to adapt our organizational structure to fit the strengths and weaknesses of our people rather than try to change our people to fit the organizational structure.

The conclusion reached was that

> People development must rank as a top priority. In a company like ours, with many executives and managers recruited from the outside, we must guard against paying lip service to this vital requirement for future growth.

Management development at General Electric

At General Electric the management development mission is expressed as:

- To ensure that the best available talent is considered for each job and that each opening is considered for its developmental potential.

- To see that there is a reasonable yet selective flow of managers across the corporation.

- To ensure that the top organization structure is consonant with long-term company objectives and strategy, and enhances top executives' development.

- To provide a competitive compensation programme to attract, retain, and motivate key employees.

The basic management philosophy driving the General Electric system of executive development is described in the following 10 main points:

1   Assuring development of managerial excellence in the company is the chief executive's most important responsibility.

2   Managers at all levels must be similarly responsible and must 'own' the development system(s).

3   Promotion from within, for motivational value, will be the rule, not the exception.

4   A key step in planning the development of managers is the manpower review process.

5   Managerial abilities are learned primarily by managing. Other activities are variable adjuncts.

6   Control of the selection process is essential in order to use openings developmentally.

7   The company can tolerate and needs a wide variety of managerial styles, traits, abilities, etc.

8   Several different managerial streams and development planning systems are needed to accommodate the company's size, diversity and decentralization.

9   Occasionally it may be necessary to distort otherwise sound compensation practice and/or change organization structure to achieve developmental results.

10 Staff people must add value in these processes but their roles are secondary to the managerial roles.

Career planning at W H Smith

Hank Bowen believes that career planning is 'a prime function of general management at all levels, assisted and guided, but never replaced, by people like myself.' He goes on to say that

> The basis of career planning must be the efficient and correct measurement of performance and potential. . . .
> However, I must now face you with an unpalatable truth. It is a fact, which must be recognized, that in any organization, no matter how large or small, half the management team will have reached their ceiling half way through their career. . . . Management succession is a pyramid *not* a ladder. It is a balance between the aspirations, ambitions, hopes of the individual and

the needs of the company for high potential, well motivated, highly trained and developed individuals, both for the present and the future. This does not mean that half the management team is on the scrap heap aged 40-plus. They have a very useful career and working life ahead of them. However, their chances of rising further in the hierarchy will be limited.

The career review procedure is designed to provide a framework within which both the individual and the company work together to make use of the individual's talents and aspirations and to assess the requirements for training and development. It is normally conducted for the top 250 managers every three years in addition to the annual performance review.
There are five sections to the review:

1 *Present facts:* i.e. educational, professional and technical qualifications, vocational and management training programmes attended, employment experience outside the company, employment within the company after a set period of years, and current job title.

2 *Personal qualities:* the individuals' perceptions of their own strengths and weaknesses.

3 *Individual future plans:* the individuals' plans and aspirations for the future.

4 *The assessment of managerial skills:* by a director or senior manager.

5 *Future intentions:* long-term possibilities of career development. These are not firm plans or intentions but a summary of possibilities that enable individuals to be trained and developed. This part is completed under divisional director guidance and remains confidential information.

The review process involves assessors (senior managers plus directors) in:

(a) agreeing or otherwise the individual's personal assessment;

(b) discussing the individual's ambitions and proposed development;

(c) grading the individual on performance in the present job;

(d) grading the individual's readiness to be promoted to the next level;

(e) commenting on the individual's aspirations;

(f) proposing any career development steps, which might include further experience in the same job or a job at the same level as well or instead of training;

(g) identifying training needs for longer-term development;

(h) indicating mid- and long-term potential and possible job moves over the next five years together with an estimate of when the manager will be able to take up his or her next job (this section is completed by directors).

Finally, career reviews for managers in the top three grades are seen by their executive director, while the chairman and the managing director see the reviews of all the top-level managers.

Human resource planning at Unilever

At Unilever, as explained by Tony Vineall, the three-man chief executive, who act as one, spend a whole day every year on a review of the human resource planning right across the company. They are concerned with a total population of approximately 20,000 managers out of the 350,000 people employed by Unilever worldwide.

> We talk very specifically about the people who are going to move into the top 200 jobs in Unilever. Further down the line we talk about the total numbers of people available for promotion and where we think the pressure points are. What they particularly look for is an overview. Not just who is available at the top, but who is coming up.
>
> I think one of the measures of our progress is that we increasingly find that there are 10 or 12 areas where we ought to be putting pressure on rather than talking in very broad generalizations. We've been able to focus on specific issues. Some years ago we talked about the need to increase the intake of high potential people and move them faster. Today, we're conscious that we have specific problems like marketing people in Germany and financial people almost everywhere.

Ten things to do to ensure that management development and career planning processes contribute effectively to the bottom line:

1 Make management development strategy an integral part of the organization's overall strategy.

2 Involve top management in the planning and review process.

3 Compel all managers to accept the total responsibility of developing their staff and helping them to advance their careers.

4 Conduct a comprehensive competency analysis.

5 Measure performance and long-term potential.

6 Maintain a balance between the aspirations, abilities and skills of individuals and the requirements of the business.

7 Emphasize the importance of self-development and help individuals to achieve a strong sense of professional direction.

8   Remember that progress is not necessarily vertical. It does, and should, include better performance in the present job and, in some cases, the ability to change from one discipline to another.

9   Do not concentrate so much on the high flyers that the middle ground is neglected.

10 Use, in accordance with the needs of the business and of the individuals concerned, an appropriate mix of development processes: for example, external or in-house training courses, coaching, counselling, planned experience, job rotation, job enrichment, open (distance) learning, guided studies, computer-based training and self-development programmes.

Reference

1   CHANDLER, A. *Strategy and structure: chapters on the history of American industrial enterprise.* Cambridge, Mass., MIT Press, 1962

12 Performance Management and the Bottom Line

WHAT IS PERFORMANCE MANAGEMENT?

Performance management is the process of guiding, appraising, developing, motivating and rewarding people to improve the results they and the organization achieve as measured ultimately by the bottom line.

Don Beattie describes the ICL 'managing for performance' programme as being:

> All about how to put into place an interlocking series of attitudes, processes and behaviours which ensure that we achieve continued improvement in the effectiveness of our human resource.
>
> It's about getting the confidence and competence in an organization to handle performance management just as thoroughly and professionally as any other aspect of running the business, and making it happen. And it's something which has eluded many organizations for many years.

THE NEED FOR PERFORMANCE MANAGEMENT

Improved performance does not just happen. It has to be managed. The process starts at the top through the articulation of corporate values and the organization's mission. These will emphasize what Sue Birley calls an 'excitement culture'[1]. The stress will be on innovation, flexibility, enterprise and rapid response to challenge and change.

The ever-increasing demands on companies to remain competitive in the face of turbulence, change and market pressures force them, in Tony Vineall's words 'to make the good better'.

> Writing the policy is fairly easy. Making it happen takes the time and the effort. We were concerned that we might go into the

156

1990s without enough people for the top jobs, so a lot of policy is focused on the high flyers, getting some of the best graduates and moving them fast.

It's now becoming clear, and I have seen this elsewhere, that it's not just a question of high flyers. Because of the overall shortage and pressures, and because of the demographic facts of life in Europe over the next five years, we all realize that there has to be a huge exercise in making the good better. What's got to happen nationally is that we must take the people in the tenth percentile and move them up to what the level above them are doing, and then continue the process and upgrade at every level.

That's true at the mega level but it's also true inside a company. It's not only important to get the people who are moving fast to go to the top. The requirements are going up everywhere and that puts great pressure on the personnel function to upgrade performance at all levels.

Performance management extends, therefore, to all categories of staff. It does this by integrating a number of personnel processes into a coherent strategy for adding value and improving results. It is also, in Don Beattie's words:

An essential contributor to a massive and urgent change programme in an organization.

THE PERFORMANCE MANAGEMENT PROCESS

Performance management is geared to achieving the short and longer term goals of the enterprise by integrating the following processes:

- *Culture change:* developing an entrepreneurial and performance conscious culture.

- *Resourcing:* obtaining and developing people who will perform effectively within the culture.

- *Guiding:* making sure that people are fully aware of their accountabilities, the critical success factors or criteria, the results they are expected to attain, the best ways of achieving these results and the competences they must have to perform effectively.

- *Appraising:* reviewing and measuring performance by comparing achievements against goals, expressed as targets, standards of performance or tasks to be completed, and by assessing competence in relation to job requirements.

- *Performance improvement:* on the basis of appraisals, helping people to improve their performance by counselling, coaching and training.

- *Motivating:* encouraging people to work more effectively by any of the financial or non-financial means available.

- *Reward management:* developing competitive pay systems and paying for performance, thus providing incentives and rewards which channel endeavours and effort in the right directions.

Culture change

The starting point is to develop a performance orientated culture.

The organization has not only to set demanding standards of performance and insist on their achievement, it also has to create the environment in which performance can be improved. For example, as Sue Birley[2] suggests, it can encourage entrepreneurship by such means as:

- loosening the reins

- reducing bureaucratic reporting requirements

- creating smaller strategic business units which are closer to the market and run by 'hands on' managers

- rewarding success rather than penalizing failure.

Resourcing

Resourcing for performance means following the principles described in the last chapter, but stressing even more strongly the performance requirements when planning recruitment and human resource development programmes. This is not a matter of simply looking at inputs to performance expressed in the shape of competency standards; nor is it a question of concentrating on expected behaviours and the activities which have to be carried out. What it does mean is an emphasis on outputs and accountabilities for results.

In their analysis of strategic orientations, Miles and Snow[3] classified organizations into four types:

1 *Prospector* – where the emphasis is on effectiveness

2 *Defender* – where the emphasis is on efficiency

3 *Analyzer* – which is a combination of one and two

4 *Reactor* – where there is no consistent or coherent strategy.

The most successful companies in the longer term are those that are more profit conscious than cost conscious and invest their way out of problems rather than concentrating on cost reduction. These, in Miles and Snow typology, are the prospector companies and they need managers who:

- are orientated to problem finding rather than problem solving

- are market orientated, with competences in product and market research and development

- are strategic thinkers

- can manage ambiguity

- create structure rather than manage it

- take calculated risks

- can when necessary ignore the rules.

At all levels the prospector type company needs to find people who will respond quickly and flexibly to challenge and change, who will accept demanding assignments gladly, and who recognize the congruence between their own interests and those of the organization. In its turn, the organization must pay continuing attention to their development, motivation and reward and to giving them the opportunity to progress with the company so that people can say 'We don't have jobs here, we have careers.'

Guiding

Casey Stengel, Manager of the New York Yankees once said:

> If you don't know where you're going, you might end up somewhere else.

A truism of course, but it is a fact that people can get lost on the route towards better performance unless they understand what they are expected to achieve (objectives) and how their achievements will be measured (success criteria). And it is also a fact that in many organizations these objectives and criteria are never clarified. Don Beattie conducted an attitude survey of ICL employees some years ago and noted that:

> One particularly salient question was 'My manager regularly shows me how to improve my performance.' Less than one-third of our employees thought that this was the case. And so there was very clearly something fundamentally wrong with the relationship between many of our managers and those they managed. There was not a unanimity of purpose and cohesion of working relationship between boss and subordinate of the sort that we would like to think we had.
> Our future direction led us to the determination that we were going to address the whole question of performance management. We recognized that there were likely to be a number of strands in effective performance management. We broke it down into four principal areas. The first of these was to establish how effective we were in explaining to our employees what was

expected of them. Here such issues as individual objective setting and job performance standards feature. When we looked, we found we were patchy on objective setting and many of our job descriptions were not clear on the *outputs* that were needed.

The other three performance management areas referred to by Don Beattie were:

- the need to have technical career structures rather than individual job descriptions for the large number of technical specialists employed by ICL;

- the whole issue of appraisal – 'setting objectives is fine but there must be an effective feedback loop';

- the pay system itself, which needed to focus on the necessary incentives and rewards.

Objective setting and accountabilities

The concept of management by objectives as devised by Peter Drucker, has, of course, been around a long time. And the idea of 'accountable management' was introduced to the Civil Service by the Fulton Committee in the late 1960s. But management by objectives as a system has become somewhat discredited, partly because the orginal schemes often sank under the weight of their paperwork and partly because there was too much emphasis on quantified objectives and too little recognition of the fact that quantified results can be affected by circumstances beyond the job-holder's control. The concept of accountable management has also tended to fade away, perhaps because of the resistance of some higher civil servants to the idea of being held to account in particular ways for what they are supposed to achieve.

But the principle of holding people to account for the achievement of specified objectives remains inviolate, so long as the following 10 guidelines are borne in mind:

1 Individual job objectives should be congruent with departmental objectives, which should in turn be derived from corporate objectives.

2 Objectives should be stated as expected outputs in terms of:
   - quantified targets or budgets, where possible;
   - standards of performance, which define when job holders and their managers know that the objective has been achieved – that the job has been done well;
   - tasks or projects to be accomplished within a given period of time which have to achieve specified results.

3 The objectives should be related to defined key result areas or principal accountabilities. They should be achievable but not too easily. In other words, people should be stretched by their objectives but not too

far. For managerial, professional and technical staff objectives should be set both for the short and the longer term. They should encompass strategic goals as well as immediate results.

4   In setting objectives, external factors beyond the employee's control should be taken into account.

5   The principal accountabilities or key result areas against which output requirements are specified should be limited in number. For some jobs, no more than three or four need be set. The number should not normally reach double figures.

6   Success criteria and performance measures should be established for each principal accountability or key results area.

7   Agreement should be reached between job holders and their managers or supervisors on the principal accountabilities or key result areas, on short-term objectives, targets and standards of performance, on longer-term goals, and on success criteria.

8   As appropriate, agreement should also be reached on the actions required to achieve objectives and the competences needed to meet performance standards. However, discussions to reach such agreements should be limited to areas where it is clear that guidance is needed. Managers should allow as much scope as possible to subordinates for them to make their own decisions and to operate as flexibly as possible within the framework of overall objectives. How much freedom can be allowed obviously depends on the circumstances, which include the nature of the work and the experience and competence of the subordinate.

9   Managers should make sure that their subordinates have the resources needed to achieve their objectives. These will include people, money, materials, equipment and, importantly, time. It should, however, always be remembered that effective management is often about making the best use of limited resources.

10   The paperwork required to support the objectives setting system should be kept to a minimum.

Performance appraisal

Aims
In general, all appraisal schemes aim to improve performance. In the National Health Service, the specific aims of the individual performance review process introduced by Len Peach are stated as being to provide:

- an opportunity for the individual to know what performance is expected of him/her and to receive feedback;
- a considered means of monitoring career needs and opportunities;

- a chance to develop a common culture of NHS values relating to performance and improved patient care.

Apart from patient care, these are typical of most schemes.

Basic outputs

The basic outputs from a performance appraisal system as in ICL are:

1   A factual statement of what has been achieved against the previous period's objectives;

2   An analysis of strengths and weaknesses against the key criteria for the job;

3   A statement of the training and personal development programmes needed to improve performance in the present job;

4   An assessment of the longer term career aspirations of the employees and an estimate of their career aiming point (where they might ultimately go) and their next likely step and its timing.

Achievement rating

The traditional results orientated approach starts with the agreement of objectives. Periodically, a factual statement of what has been achieved against these objectives is agreed by managers and their subordinates. The latter are encouraged to assess their own performance first, which is then compared with their manager's assessment. The discussion includes an analysis of the reasons why certain results have been obtained. New or revised objectives and action plans for the next period are then discussed and agreed.

Some systems, such as that used in the National Health Service, take achievements against a scale, which in the NHS consists of five bands:

Band 1   Consistently exceeds short-term objectives and makes excellent progress towards long-term goals

Band 2   Exceeds some short-term objectives and makes good progress towards long-term goals

Band 3   Meets all short-term objectives and makes fairly good progress towards long-term goals

Band 4   Meets most short-term objectives and makes satisfactory progress towards long-term goals

Band 5   Meets few short-term objectives and makes little or no progress towards long-term goals.

An overall rating is then given, using this scale and based on the ratings allocated to the individual objectives.

Analysis of strengths and weaknesses
Some appraisal schemes concentrate on the results orientated approach and do not attempt to assess behaviour. The reasoning behind this is sound. Whereas behaviour cannot be quantified or measured, results can. If care is not taken managers get involved in assessing the personality traits of their subordinates, which must be a totally subjective exercise. Enthusiasm, energy, self-confidence and loyalty can generate a favourable image, although people with all these characteristics can still be poor performers.

On the other hand, it can be argued convincingly that performance improvement is only feasible if individuals know where they need to increase their competences and which types of behaviour are likely to achieve better results. The starting point must still be the measurement of achievements against objectives, but to analyze additionally *how* the results were obtained and thus point the way to the future can be a most effective way of increasing the effectiveness of individuals and hence their contribution to the bottom line.

A competency approach involves setting out the competences required for a job in terms of the skills and behaviours needed for its satisfactory performance. Skills and behaviours are described in terms of the actual and observable things people have to be able to do.

This aspect of the appraisal process works best if agreement is reached between managers and their subordinates on the competences required. This agreement should be made when setting objectives and can be revised as necessary following the performance review. Gaps and weaknesses can then be identified, to be filled or overcome as part of the performance improvement plan.

The personnel function has an important part to play in these processes. Managers and their staff need to be trained in competency analysis and assessment. Help is often required in developing the basic lists of competences from personnel professionals who can use job and skills analysis techniques. The personnel function can create and maintain a database of competences for each job in the organization.

A competency approach has been developed by Cadbury Schweppes using a model based on capability, eligibility and suitability.

- *Capability* – measures the overall calibre, capacity, intellect and potential of the individual;

- *Eligibility* – examines the technical or professional skills, knowledge and experience that the individual possesses;

- *Suitability* – identifies the distinctive behaviour, style, attitudes and values which will determine the individual's ability 'to fit the unique interpersonal chemistry of the particular work situation'.

This model has been used in Cadbury Schweppes to build a database which is achieving demonstrable success in promoting more careful and imaginative placement, in building both effective teams and boss/subordinate combinations and in helping people to grow. A competency dictionary was developed which identified 50 discrete behaviours and clustered them under six broad headings. This made it possible to convey in managerial terms the distinctive shape of an individual for whom a comprehensive profile is built up from all available data sources and amended as new information becomes available.

Training and development needs
Training and development needs, as identified by the review process (objectives and competences), can be set out in a personal development plan which, as in the NHS scheme, describes against each objective any learning or development needs and the proposed actions.

Career development
Career development plans are derived from analyses of the aspirations expressed by employees, and assessments of potential in relation to the future human resource requirements of the company as set out in its strategic plans. The performance appraisal system should therefore provide people with the opportunity both to express and to discuss their aspirations. In so far as these are realistic, development plans can then be evolved and implemented.

Performance appraisal: 10 requirements for success
The performance appraisal system should:

1   Adopt a results orientated approach, i.e. it should be based on the assessment of achievements against agreed objectives;

2   Involve the analysis and assessment of competences as well as achievements;

3   Be seen as the basis for constructive dialogues between managers and their subordinates, not as a generator of paper;

4   Be seen as part of the normal process of management at all levels in the organization, not just a routine imposed by the personnel department;

5   Make sure that all involved understand that performance appraisal dialogues should be positive, supportive and forward looking – forums for exploring new ideas and improving performance rather than means of generating alibis and excuses;

6   Form part of regular and informal discussions about progress using agreed performance and personal development plans. Performance appraisal is not an annual event;

7   Emphasize the future – what can be done and what needs to be done – rather than dwelling on the past;

8   Encourage both managers and their subordinates to prepare carefully for the review;

9   Be supported by extensive training for all concerned on methods of

setting objectives, analyzing competency, conducting review meetings, counselling, coaching and translating plans into action;

10 Be monitored by the managers of the managers carrying out the appraisal (the 'grandfathers') as well as the personnel function to ensure that it is being carried out thoroughly, fairly and productively.

Performance improvement

From the bottom line point of view, the most important output from the appraisal process is the performance improvement plan. This describes:

1 What individuals must do for themselves to improve their performance by developing their strengths, overcoming their weaknesses, enhancing their skills and modifying their behaviour. This is the basis for self-development, which everyone agrees is the best form of development but is, in practice, the most difficult to arrange. Hence the importance of the self-appraisal and counselling aspects of the performance review.

2 What managers should do for individual members of their staff in the shape of guidance, counselling, coaching and enlarging experience.

3 What the organization can do for individuals in the form of on- or off-the-job training and development programmes and planned experience.

Motivating

Motivating strategy should be designed to maximize the effective output of employees. Its impact on the bottom line should be evidenced by increased productivity, lower costs per unit of output and better all-round performance.

The importance of expectancy theory
The strategy should be based on expectancy theory which, as formulated by two American researchers, Porter and Lawler[4], suggests that the following factors will influence effective effort and therefore performance:

● the value of rewards to individuals in so far as they satisfy their needs. The rewards can be financial or non-financial. In the latter case they may have a more powerful and longer-lasting effect if they involve one or more of the following: achievement, recognition, added responsibility, status or the acquisition of power (the last two may be undesirable but they can still be strong motivators);

● the probability that rewards depend on effort as perceived by individuals – that it, their expectations about the extent to which their efforts will produce a worthwhile reward;

- ability – individual characteristics and attributes such as intelligence, skill and knowhow;

- role perceptions – what individuals want to do and what they are required to do. These are good from the viewpoint of the organization if they correspond with what it thinks individuals ought to be doing. They are poor if the views of individuals and the organization do not coincide.

The motivation model which describes these relationships is shown in Figure 12.1.

The impact of goal theory
The motivation strategy should also be based on goal theory as developed by Locke[5]. This states that motivation and performance will be higher when:

- individuals are set specific goals

- goals are difficult but accepted

- participation between managers and subordinates takes place as a means of getting agreement to the setting of higher goals

- the achievement of difficult goals is reinforced by guidance and advice

- there is feedback on performance to maintain motivation, particularly towards reaching even higher goals.

Motivating strategy
The following 10-point motivation strategy is based on the combined messages of expectancy and goal theory.

1   Set and agree demanding goals

2   Provide feedback on performance

3   Create expectations that certain behaviours and outputs will produce worthwhile rewards when they succeed but will result in penalties if they fail

4   Design jobs which enable people to feel a sense of accomplishment, to express and use their abilities and to exercise their own decision-making powers

5   Provide appropriate tangible rewards for achievement (pay for performance)

6   Provide intangible rewards such as praise for work well done

7   Communicate to individuals and publicize generally the link between performance and reward, thus enhancing expectations

8   Select and train managers and supervisors who will exercise effective leadership and have the required motivating skills

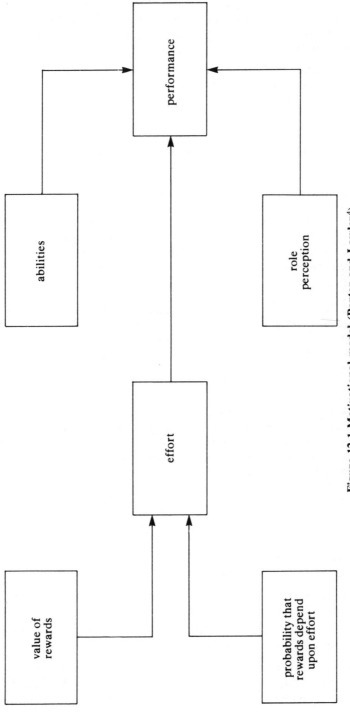

Figure 12.1 Motivational model (Porter and Lawler[4])

9   Give people the guidance and training which will develóp the knowledge, skills and understanding they need to improve their performance

10 Show individuals what they have to do to satisfy their aspirations through career progression.

Reward management

Reward management should be regarded as a strategy which is driven by business needs. As Barry Curnow said:

> Businessmen are often very frustrated with the existing structures, grading systems and pay arrangements that are in place. They are saying, 'How can I make reward do what I want it to do for me and my business?' They are challenging us to look at remuneration in a new way . . . as an active change agent, that we can really use to help our business do some of the things we want to do.

The old concept of salary administration, with its emphasis on order, systems and control has been replaced by the new concept of reward management, with its emphasis on performance, flexibility and the creation of added value from the organization's human resources by means of the pay system.

Rosabeth Moss Kanter has suggested that we must:

> Analyze and, if necessary, rethink the relationship between pay and value to the organization. Keep in mind that organizational levels defined for purposes of co-ordination do not necessarily reflect contribution to performance goals, and decouple pay from status and rank. And, finally, be prepared to justify pay decisions in terms of clear contributions – and to offer these contributions more often to more stakeholder groups.[6]

The main features of the reward management concept are:

• the pay system is market driven – external competitiveness is given priority over internal equity;

• great importance is attached to paying for performance to provide the incentive required to generate added value;

• the appeal is more to what the individual wants and needs rather than to collective demands and requirements;

• the reward system must reflect the circumstances and requirements of the organization and must be able to respond quickly and flexibly to changes in those requirements as they affect individuals;

- the trend is towards integrated pay systems in single-status organizations, although rewards will still be related to value and contribution;
- there is a move away from fringe benefits to money;
- an increasing emphasis is placed on getting added value from pay.

Reward strategy for high performance
The overall approach to reward strategy adopted by Cadbury Schweppes is as follows:

> We require a strategic approach to the design of pay and benefit systems which:
>
> - is geared to individual business strategies and practices but recognizes the increasingly international nature of our business;
> - is an integral part of an overall human resource strategy geared to those business requirements;
> - is market driven within each country, thus enabling us to attract, select and retain world-class employees;
> - is designed to motivate and reinforce superior performance;
> - is flexible and increasingly individually orientated, yet soundly constructed and providing a relevant framework and basis for proper control and reasonable equity;
> - is the subject of regular review as to its continuing relevance and effectiveness in meeting strategic business requirements;
> - provides, over and above existing national pay and benefit arrangements:
>   - an effective framework for international moves;
>   - for situations where there is multi-business presence in a particular country;
>   - for trans-national arrangements to meet business needs.

The key elements in reward strategy
The key elements in the Cadbury Schweppes reward strategy are:

1 *A basic salary structure* which is competitive in the market and in which individual salary is performance driven via regular reviews geared to the business cycle. Performance is assessed against clear and consistent standards relating to the achievement of individual business objectives and competence development.

2 *Variable pay* in the form of bonuses geared to the success fo the business. This needs to reflect the performance of the team at each

senior level of the business and also reflect achievement against annual budget.

3 *Benefit programmes* geared to local market requirements, but recognizing the multi-national nature of our business on the provision of an international share option for senior people.

How reward management can improve bottom-line performance
The following are 10 ways in which effective reward management systems can improve bottom-line performance:

1 Stimulate and direct effort towards the achievement of corporate goals for added value and competitive gain.

2 Help to develop performance-related careers and support the achievement of the objectives of the organization by conveying a clear message on the corporate values relating to entrepreneurship, innovation, endeavour and improved performance as measured by bottom-line results.

3 Underpin these values by linking rewards to accomplishment and effective effort.

4 Establish and clarify priorities for people in terms of their key result areas.

5 Attract high-quality people who fit the culture of the organization for which the reward system has been devised.

6 Ensure that high-quality staff prosper and stay with the organization.

7 Encourage enterprise, innovation and strategic thinking.

8 Avoid demotivating the people the company wishes to retain.

9 Motivate the masses as well as the high flyers.

10 Deliver the message to poor performers that they must improve or go.

How reward management systems should be designed and operated to improve bottom-line performance
The following are 10 approaches that can be adopted to make sure that in practice, reward management strategies, policies and systems, fulfil their promise of improving bottom-line results.

1 Relate pay system to organizational needs and culture.

2 Relate pay to contribution and performance.

3 Establish performance criteria.

4 Assess performance against the criteria.

5 Evaluate jobs systematically to achieve a reasonable degree of equity.

6 Monitor market rates to maintain competitiveness.

7 Segment the pay structure into market groups as required.

8 Ensure that the pay system promotes rather than discourages flexibility.

9 Communicate the message about the system and how and why it benefits employees.

10 Remember the other forms of motivation.

Paying for performance

A growing trend
From the bottom line point of view the most important aspect of the new approaches to reward management is the emphasis on performance-related pay, as was noted by Rosabeth Moss Kanter:[7]

> More and more senior executives are trying to turn their employees into entrepreneurs – people who earn a direct return on the value they help create.

Alan Fowler noted five main trends.[8]

1 A move away from the emphasis on personal qualities inherent in conventional merit rating towards the assessment of performance against working objectives.

2 The widespread introduction of performance pay into the public sector, partly because performance pay has become an important feature of the Government's plans for achieving a more commercial or managerial attitude within the public services, and partly because some local authorities have seen the improvements in efficiency which can result from systematic performance management.

3 An extension of performance appraisal and pay from the managerial sector to employees generally, including, in some cases, clerical and manual workers. British Airways and Abbey National, for example, now pay all their white-collared staff on a performance basis. This trend is associated with the move towards single status firms.

4 The abandonment of a general, annual pay increase for all staff with additional individual merit payments, substituted by systems in which all increases are decided on an individual performance basis. Beginning in 1985, for example, Ford has been extending wholly merit-based pay increases from a very small number of the most senior managers, first to middle management, then with a planned extension to junior managers and supervisors in 1990. Alan Fowler notes, however, that it is still necessary to keep pay in line with market

rates, which would mean additional across the board increases or, possibly, increases to selected market groups. He also noted that this approach is most applicable in periods of low inflation and depends, where they exist, on trade union acquiescence. And although many trade unions, even in the public sector, have abandoned their traditional opposition to merit pay, there is no certainty that they will go on doing so.

5   An increasing sophistication or complexity in both the performance appraisal process and the statistical calculation of performance payments. Shell and British Airways, for example, use ranking systems to construct a hierarchy of performance levels.

The British Airways scheme, which assesses performance against both the achievement of objectives and some 60 management practices or competences, has to be processed by computer to produce a score for each employee. This score shows, in effect, where each employee stands in relation to the performance of all the others. From this an individual maximum salary target is set, and an exponential salary curve is charted towards the target. In the National Westminster Bank, too, salary progression is on an exponential curve for employees who consistently achieve the same performance rating.

Performance related pay schemes can use a simple approach incorporating incremental salary scales or a 'spot rate' salary structure (fixed salary points), and pay a lump-sum bonus in addition to the increment or above the spot rate. A more complex approach, used by some organizations like IBM, with a salary range system where there are no incremental scales, is to have variable rates of progression through the range related to an overall grading of performance. Ferranti, however, who have used this system for many years have abandoned it for a more flexible approach which does not rely upon a linkage to overall gradings.

There is a view that it is invidious to put people in boxes, with A, B, C, D or E inscribed on the lid, in which they have to live for the next year; especially if the process of encapsulating people into grades is still a subjective one, however results-orientated the system is.

All performance pay systems adopt some form of budgeting for the overall cost of the performance-related pay increases. This is, or should be, related to the performance of the company as measured by the bottom line. The link between pay and corporate performance is thus made explicit.

However, the transition of the budgeted overall increase to individual awards is done in a number of different ways, some more sophisticated than others. There are companies which use a forced distribution process; so many staff get the average increase of, say, five per cent, so many get an increase of, say, eight per cent, and so on. But as Alan Fowler points out:[9]

The only real argument for performance pay is that it helps to raise performance standards throughout the workforce. In a

successful scheme, therefore, the proportion of employees
assessed as being in the higher of the performance categories
ought, over time, to increase – which makes nonsense of forced
distributions.

Personnel managers seem very ambivalent about this. Many
expound the virtues of their schemes but become very worried if
they see an upward drift in assessments. But, if all a scheme does
is to perpetuate a natural distribution of performance standards,
it would not seem to be having any effect whatsoever.

The Alliance and Leicester Building Society operates what it calls its
'PLOP' scheme – 'percentage level of performance'. A 0–200 per cent
performance rating scale is used to determine what percentage of a
budgeted average increase should be paid. With 100 per cent as the
expected level of performance, a 95 per cent rating results in 95 per cent of
the budgeted percentage being paid, and so on.

The Abbey National scheme
The Abbey National scheme was introduced because for some time it had
been the Society's desire to link rewards more closely to individual performance. It had generally been accepted that too small a proportion of a
person's pay increase was dependent on merit and that this element was
largely swamped by the larger overall cost-of-living increase.

In changing to a performance-based scheme the Society sought to achieve
three major benefits.

1 Increased motivation towards the Society's objectives.

2 Greater perceived equity in rewards by ensuring that those who made
the greatest contribution were rewarded most.

3 Retention of better performers by providing quicker salary progression
for high achievers.

In order to achieve these benefits the following features were built into the
scheme:

- a clear and unambiguous link between performance and reward;

- a basic, consistent core;

- judgements based on a thorough and objective system of measuring
performance;

- safeguards such as management reviews and appeal systems to avoid
unfairness.

The scheme operates within a budget which is determined on the basis of
the assessments managers give to their staff. There are five performance

bands and the relationship between each band is as follows:

- unacceptable   nil
- less than effective   50%
- effective   100%
- highly effective   150%
- outstanding   200%

The budget is fixed by reference to the performance levels which managers allocate to their staff. This leads to the calculation of benchmark increases for each job grade which, however, can be tuned by managers to increase 'ownership' of the rises awarded and to recognize the fact that there is a range of performance within each band. The discretion range is plus or minus 20 per cent of the benchmark increase. Thus managers can vary a benchmark increase of, say, £1000 for effective performers between £800 and £1200, but such variations have to be made within their total budget.

Executive reward strategy
The executive remuneration strategy has to be designed to recognize the considerable individual contribution that senior directors and managers can make to the bottom line.

The ICL approach was to develop a sharply focussed high leverage plan which would help to pull the organization together. ICL, because of the highly integrated nature of its organization, needs to have a group of managers with shared and interlocking objectives. Without them, as Don Beattie says, 'the organization would fly apart.'

The main features of the ICL strategy are:

- base salary slightly below the market;

- on-target incentive earnings to produce total cash payments ahead of the market, with significant over-achievement potential on top;

- long-term incentives – typically share options – to focus people's attention on the longer-term health of the company;

- benefits broadly market competitive.

There are three, sometimes two, elements, to the plan for executives. First, all executives have a portion of their bonus derived from the achievement of company results. Secondly, for line executives, a portion of their bonus is related to the results of their own operation. This is not available to staff executives. Thirdly, there are personal objectives geared to the longer-term strategic direction of the company.

The ICL approach is typical of many well conceived schemes, but there are almost infinite variations. Executive incentive schemes can create problems if they do not fairly relate reward to performance.

Paying for performance: the issues

Paying for performance raises issues:

1 Does it work, and if so how?

2 What is the relationship between performance appraisal and the reward?

3 How can the scheme be made to operate fairly?

4 How can its impact be extended throughout the organization?

5 How should it be introduced?

Does it work?
Paying for performance sounds like a good idea. It is generally believed that it will improve results because it acts as a major form of incentive and, in any case, it seems fair to pay people more for doing better, and less for doing worse.

However, a word of caution may be necessary. Instinctively, we feel that performance will improve if appropriate financial incentives and rewards are provided. But is this belief supported by incontrovertible evidence derived from research and analysis? On the shop floor perhaps (although some cast doubt on this), but at management level one cannot be so certain.

Extensive research carried out recently at Oxford University by Margaret Ellis of Sainsburys failed to reveal any convincing evidence supporting a direct, specific and continuing relationship between the level of performance-related reward and performance.

The only research she could turn up was carried out in the United States by Pearce, Stevenson and Derry in 1983. This studied the impact of introducing what they called 'performance-contingent compensation' in the Social Security Administration. Rigorous analysis provided no evidence that it had any significant effect on performance.

It has been argued that contingent pay plans should be avoided because they reduce intrinsic motivation, lead individuals to develop strategies that will enable them to get rewards with least effort, and can easily break down, if, for instance 'no-one is looking'.

One piece of negative research and the above argument do not, of course, destroy the case for performance-related pay. It is powerful. It is persuasive. But it is still worth asking ourselves if the claims that it is a sort of 'universal panacea' are really justified. The argument that 'everyone is doing it' is not always a good one. In this connection it is worth remembering that there is a fair amount of evidence from research that many, if not most managers have relatively little control over corporate results. It has been suggested that managerial actions can account for as little as 10 per cent of the variance in organizational performance.

Perhaps this is an over-pessimistic view, but we all know that the results achieved by an individual can be greatly affected by circumstances beyond his or her control. And this will damage the key relationship that must exist between effort and results if performance-related pay is going to work.

In any case, are we sure that we are right in appealing to greed? Do we really subscribe to the view of Gordon Gekko in *Wall Street* (a hero for our times if ever there was one) whose manifesto was:

> Greed is good. Greed works. Greed clarifies, cuts through and captures the essence of the evolutionary spirit.

The problem we may face in nurturing 'Graspies' (get rich as soon as possible people) is that they may grasp the wrong thing.

This is not by any means to dismiss the concept of paying for performance, which clearly is a most attractive one. Even if it does not make people work *harder* it should at least contribute to making them work more effectively by highlighting key performance areas. And the fact that a company has such systems is a good way of communicating what sort of business it is. But we must not expect too much and we must make sure before we go too far that we set targets that are firmly based on business needs, are measurable and relate to key areas of individual accountability.

Relationship between appraisal and reward

Purists have argued for some time that there should not be a direct relationship between performance appraisals and rewards. The point they stress is that the main purpose of the performance review is 'developmental', that is, it is there to identify training and development needs in order to improve performance. It is said that mixing this up with pay will distort the system. People will be more concerned about how much or how little they can get out of the review and will not be receptive to the counselling that is an essential part of the process.

This is an understandable argument, but, if it is accepted that pay is going to be related to performance, it is an unrealistic one. Terry Murphy's comments on this point were:

> We didn't follow a traditional line and separate them (appraisal and reward). We said that they were clearly going to be part of the same thing. I can't believe that anyone can argue consistently that performance appraisal can be separated from reward. To me it's a nonsense. It's a nice theory.

Len Peach believes that it is still possible to de-synchronize the two systems in some circumstances, as at IBM, and get the benefits of both. This involves referring back to the performance assessment from the reward review. But he noted that:

> My experience at IBM was that people would associate their rating for performance with their rating for pay. Some research has been done in this field which shows that about 60 per cent of the companies surveyed never associate the two directly. I think

this is an area where you have to consider whether separating them is solely an idealistic viewpoint which is no longer tenable.

Achieving fairness
It may be fair to reward people according to their performance but this depends on assessing performance accurately and fairly. Measurement will always be a problem because some degree of subjective judgement is inevitable, however much stress is placed on assessing results against agreed objectives or performance against agreed standards. The only ways to minimize unfairness are; first to train managers thoroughly in setting objectives and reviewing achievements; secondly, to monitor the performance of managers as appraisers (and make their ability to appraise fairly one of the standards they have to meet); thirdly, to provide for a check on appraisals by the manager's manager (the grandfather) and, finally, to build an appeals system into the scheme and ensure that it works.

Extending coverage
Paying for performance systems aim to improve all-round organizational performance. They are not there simply to benefit the favoured few, even if these individuals can make more impact on the bottom line (for which they should be rewarded appropriately). It follows that performance-related pay should be extended as far as possible throughout the organization.

Introducing performance-related pay
Performance-related pay systems are not an easy option. They take time and care to introduce and it is easy to get them wrong. Conventional wisdom suggests that it is best to get the performance appraisal scheme off the ground before venturing into the jungle of paying for performance. But circumstances – for example, the urgent need to develop a performance-orientated culture – may dictate the simultaneous introduction of a complete performance management system as Len Peach discovered in the National Health Service.

Whatever type of system is used, and there is plenty of choice, it must be appropriate to the business and must be clearly related to the goals of the enterprise and its key result areas. It must be seen as providing leverage on these key results, which means ensuring that at each level measurable success criteria are integrated with those of the business as a whole.

Check list: performance-related pay (PRP)

General

1   What are the objectives of PRP?

2   To what extent is the principle of PRP congruent with the organization's culture and its value system?

3   Is PRP likely to be welcomed at each level in the organization and by the trade unions, if any?

Performance measures

 4 To what extent have performance criteria in the shape of objectives, targets and standards been established for different categories of staff?

 5 For which type of jobs will it be possible to quantify objectives and measure results accordingly?

 6 For jobs where the quantification of objectives is not possible, are there other methods of setting performance measures relating to the completion of projects or tasks satisfactorily or the achievement of performance standards?

Performance appraisal system

 7 Is a system of performance appraisal operated anywhere in the organization? If so:
    (a) to whom does it apply?
    (b) what type of scheme?
    (c) what is its purpose?
    (d) how effective is it?
    (e) is it likely to provide information which could be used to determine the level of PRP?

Pay system

 8 What types of pay structure exist?

 9 How is pay progressed within the system?

10 What criteria are used to determine increments?

11 If merit awards or bonus payments are made:
    (a) who gets them?
    (b) on what basis are they paid?
    (c) what is the average and the maximum payment made?

Performance-related pay system

12 Which categories of staff should be included in a PRP system and why?

13 What criteria should be used for each category to decide on the level of PRP?

14 Are these criteria relevant, measurable and fair?

15 How, in each case, will performance be measured against the criteria?

16 Who will be responsible for assessing performance and deciding on the reward?

17 Is the link between performance and reward clear?

18 Will the scheme help to establish priority performance areas?

19 Is the scheme likely to make a significant impact on individual and organizational performance?

20 Will the scheme help to develop a performance orientated culture throughout the organization?

References

1 BIRLEY, Sue. Presentation at the International Personnel Conference. The Management Centre Europe. March, 1987
2 *Ibid.*
3 MILES, R. E. *and* SNOW, C. C. *Organizational strategy, structure and purpose.* New York, McGraw Hill, 1978
4 PORTER, L. W. *and* LAWLER, E. E. *Managerial attitudes and performance.* Holmwood, Illinois, Irwin-Dorsey, 1968
5 LOCKE, F. A. 'Goal setting, a technique that works'. *Organizational Dynamics.* August, 1979
6 KANTER, Rosabeth Moss. *The change masters.* London, Allen & Unwin, 1984
7 *Ibid.*
8 FOWLER, Alan. 'New directions in performance pay'. *Personnel Management.* November, 1988 pp 30–34
9 *Ibid.*

13 Quality and Customer Care

THE NEED FOR TOTAL QUALITY AND CUSTOMER CARE

Competitive edge is built and sustained in many ways: by innovation, by aggressive marketing, by efficiency in manufacturing, distribution or the provision of a service, by top level, inspirational leadership, by effective performance management and by developing a highly competent and fully involved workforce. Transcending all these, however, is the need for everyone in the organization to pursue excellence in all they do, this means the generation of total commitment to quality and a determination to achieve high levels of customer service.

The President and Chief executive officer of Hewlett-Packard, John Young, has said that:

> In today's competitive environment, ignoring the quality issue is tantamount to corporate suicide.

Peter Wickens has noted that the Japanese have no word for quality. Instead, they use the word 'kaizen', meaning 'continuous improvement by all the staff at all times'.[1]

Production rather than market orientation was perhaps inevitable in the middle years of this century when the determinants of commercial success were mainly price and availability in the marketplace. But markets became saturated, consumerism emerged as a living and powerful force, and buying points in many markets reduced in number with a resulting shift of influence to the retailer. In global markets, the provision of maximum choice to customers became a favoured weapon in the fight for competitive advantage.

Product life cycles are shrinking. Businesses had to become market driven, to recognize that 'the customer is king'. And what customers demand is quality, in terms of both the product itself and the services provided by the organization. Businesses have had to recognize that they can only thrive and survive by delivering quality to their customers.

180

Quality has to be designed into the product or service. It has to be delivered through the processes of development, manufacturing, distribution, selling and any other contact with customers. It has to be sustained through after sales service. People do all these things, so quality is utterly dependent on them. Quality is much more of a mind set than a matter of control mechanisms.

The personnel function can bring to bear all its creativity to make quality and customer service come alive to employees. These skills are deployed in the planning and implementation of organization-wide training and communications programmes which aim to create commitment as well as teach the required skills.

TOTAL QUALITY IMPROVEMENT

What it is

Total quality improvement is an intensive, long-term effort directed at the creation and maintenance of the high standards of product quality and services expected by customers. The object is significantly to increase the awareness of all employees that quality is vital to the organization's success and their future. The business must be transformed into a unit which exists to deliver value to customers by satisfying their needs.

It has been suggested by Schneier, Baird and Beatty that the keys to successful total quality improvement (TQI) are:[2]

- measure quality

- determine the cost of quality

- incorporate quality objectives into strategic plans

- build TQI into accountabilities of every job and into all related systems (e.g. performance appraisal)

- form quality teams which are integrated, top to bottom and bottom to top, as well as laterally to include suppliers and customers

- obtain demonstrable commitment from top management

- build skills through training

- recognize and reward quality improvement.

What it isn't

Total quality improvement is not a 'programme', which implies a finite beginning and end. It is, in fact, a continuous performance.

However, although the emphasis on quality can never be relaxed, quality improvement is not simply a matter of demanding ever-increasing quality target levels, thus implying that acceptable quality is unattainable. This is a defeatist approach. Neither is it a matter of using quality control and inspection systems and expecting that these alone will improve quality, although they have their uses as monitoring and measuring devices. Total quality is not achieved by techniques such as quality circles which, as Peter Wickens says, are no more than 'a fine tuning mechanism for companies whose quality is already good'.

Quality is an attitude of mind which leads to appropriate behaviours and actions. It has to be, as at Nissan, 'the centrepiece of the company's philosophy, with commitment *at every level* to a zero-defect product.'

Total quality improvement at Philips

The company-wide quality improvement (CWQI) initiative at Philips, as described by Kees van Ham,[3] began in 1983 with a statement to all staff from the President, Dr Dekker, the central message of which was that the quality of products and services is of the utmost importance for the continuity of the company and: 'The Board of Management has decided to give vigorous direction to a company-wide approach to quality improvement.'

There were three driving forces at Philips for total quality and total performance improvement: first the market, where customers were rightly becoming more and more demanding, secondly, the competition, especially from Japan where high quality was axiomatic and, thirdly, costs, where the introduction of completely new ways of managing, organizing and working could not only increase quality but should also reduce expense.

The eight guiding principles for company-wide quality improvement at Philips are:

1   *Customer satisfaction.* The objective is to achieve a complete interface between company performance and customer needs in all aspects that customers consider to be important.

2   *Total involvement.* The total involvement of all employees at all levels is a basic condition for achieving the objective. Equally important is the complete involvement of all suppliers of goods and services.

3   *Integrated approach.* Breakthrough improvement can only be realized by a systematic approach. The start is the direction given by the strategy which is translated into objectives and the setting of clear priorities, followed by planning and implementing improvement projects, and by monitoring progress.

4   *Systematic approach.* Breakthrough improvement can only be realized by a systematic approach. The start is: direction given by strategy, translated into objectives and clear priority setting, followed by planning and implementing improvement projects and monitoring progress.

5   *Continuous improvement.* The Philips approach is not a campaign or a project. Excellence can only be achieved by continuously investing in improvement, step by step, year after year, in a never ending succession of plan-do-check-act cycles.

6 *Defect prevention.* Prevent defects from occurring. Prevent the expenditure of money on unnecessary or faulty activities. Implant a new culture of work-effectiveness and added value into the total organization.

7 *Maximum quality.* The ultimate aim is to become perfect by meeting customer needs in all aspects. This means striving for maximum total quality.

8 *Education, training and promotion.* Much more attention has to be paid to education, training and promotion. The new work culture can only be realized if people are better than ever prepared for their contribution.

CUSTOMER CARE PROGRAMMES

Total quality improvement processes aim to improve all aspects of quality, although the focus is always on satisfying customer needs. Customer care programmes concentrate on the levels of service provided by the organization as an important aspect of total quality. This covers the services provided to customers at the order processing or fulfilment (selling) stage, which includes all personal contacts with customers, as well as after sales service.

Nick Cowan emphasized the significance of customer care:

> Customer care programmes are tremendously important in a service industry – it's really the only competitive element. They can range from one-day 'smile' courses right through to a fundemantal shift in the culture of the organization. And good personnel management is absolutely fundamental, because good customer care is about the competence, confidence and calibre of staff.
>
> Research in the United States has shown that the level of customer service depends first of all on what the level of service the staff *think* they are giving. If you *think* you are giving good service then you probably *are* giving good service. The second thing customer service depends on is the perception of staff about what management wants. And the important thing is that this is about the staff's perception about what management *really* wants, not about what management *says* it wants. If they say that customer care is important and all their actions involve large scale cost reductions at the expense of the customer, then you don't get customer care. The third factor is the calibre of personnel management in the organization. It is almost as if the people in contact with customers are transparent so that customers can see through them and observe the quality of personnel management on matters such as pay, support given to the people in the front line and the environment which has been created for them to work in.

Customer service is a continuous process and although it is usually described as a programme, this is misleading if it implies that it consists of a limited campaign.

Customer care programmes recognize that customer choice is increasingly being determined by the perceived level of service the business provides for them. They are also based on the understanding that quality and service are the main factors which generate customer loyalty – to the product or to the brand. An enterprise wants to obtain good business from its customers but it also wants repeat business.

The general principles governing the improvement of levels of customer care and service are similar to those for total quality improvement, namely:

1 The drive for customer care must be led from the top.

2 Customer care must be accepted and 'owned' by management at all levels as something which will lead to specific and measurable improvements in organizational performance and the bottom line.

3 Actions speak louder than words. Anything that management does which affects customer service, however remotely (and this means just about everything), should be seen by all concerned as part of a continuous improvement process.

4 The concept of customer care and all that it implies must be spread to all levels of the organization. A 'cascade' approach is usually best if it generates commitment and action at each level, which can be passed on down the organization.

5 The approach to developing constructive, positive and profitable attitudes towards customer care must make the customer come alive for all employees. This involves making the points as strongly as possible that 'real people are counting on us to do our jobs well' and that 'every contact with a customer is an opportunity to add value and quality'.

6 Explicitly identify and strengthen all customer connections.

7 Bear in mind that all employees are also customers, so that messages about customer service can be presented to them as real concerns which they have to live with, rather than abstractions such as productivity and profitability. They know when they are getting value as customers and the concept of added value can therefore easily be made real to them.

8 Establish direct links between what every function does and its impact on the customer. This includes those which are not in direct contact with customers. In fact, particular care should be taken to include them. Having established the links, analyze the attitudes and skills required to provide better customer care and assess the degree to which the attitudes exist and the skills are practised. Any gaps identified between actual and desired behaviour define a training need.

9   Remember that doing things better generally means doing things differently. Improving levels of customer service involves cultural change. This is not achieved easily or quickly. One or two day seminars and a lot of sloganizing are not enough. Continuing effort is required to produce commitment to customer care and to make significant changes for the better in attitudes and behaviour.

10 The impact of customer care on performance and on customer attitudes and buying behaviour must be measured. Success criteria should be set and results monitored against these criteria in direct bottom-line terms or by means of customer research and attitude surveys.

The W H Smith approach

The W H Smith approach to customer care, called 'First Service' exemplifies the principle that everybody in the organization should be involved. This includes recognizing the need to treat colleagues as customers.
   The four objectives of 'First Service' are:

1   An open participative management style;

2   Effective communications systems at all levels;

3   Recognition of colleagues and the public as customers;

4   Development, implementation and monitoring of performance standards designed to achieve excellence in service, quality and efficiency.

The First Service approach places great emphasis on defining for each aspect of customer care the success criteria, how performance will be measured and how it will be monitored. These, and the actions required to meet the criteria, are disseminated through a comprehensive training programme.

THE CONTRIBUTION OF THE PERSONNEL FUNCTION

The personnel function is ideally placed to make a major contribution to total quality improvement and customer care. Improvements in these areas mean influencing the attitudes and behaviour of employees. Cultural change is involved.
   To achieve this requires research and analysis of present attitudes, beliefs and competences and the development and implementation of relevant education, training, communication and performance appraisal programmes. All these are within the remit of the personnel function which has, or should have, the skills and the independence required to support and help implement top management's total quality improvement mission.

As Nick Cowan put it:

> When you get into customer care you get into the whole culture of the organization. This means that personnel directors are riding into the basic philosophy of the company. And this is inevitable when you think it's about people – their selection, training, career progression and organization. In this area the personnel director can contribute directly to the bottom line by providing what Karen Legge calls 'unique, non-substitutable expertise'.

References

1 WICKENS, Peter. *The road to Nissan*. London, Macmillan, 1987

2 SCHNEIER, Craig, BAIRD, Lloyd *and* BEATTY, Richard. 'Total quality improvement becomes reality through performance management'. *The performance management sourcebook*. Amherst, Mass., Human Resource Development Press, 1987

3 VAN HAM, Kees. 'Total quality improvement'. Address to the MCE International Personnel Management Conference, Lisbon, 1987

14   Gaining Commitment

WHAT IS COMMITMENT?

Commitment denotes three areas of feeling or behaviour related to the company in which a person works.

1   Belief in, and acceptance of, the organization itself and its goals and values

2   Willingness to go 'beyond the normal call of duty' in working for the organization

3   Desire to remain a member of the organization.

Commitment is a wider concept than motivation and tends to be more stable over a period of time. It is less responsive to transitory aspects of an employee's job. It is possible to be dissatisfied with a particular feature of a job while retaining a reasonably high level of commitment to the organization as a whole.

Commitment to the organization increases in line with the extent to which people identify with its values, goals and activities and believe that if the organization thrives, so will they. It will be maintained if people feel that they are treated fairly and are given every opportunity to use and develop their skills.

COMMITMENT AND THE BOTTOM LINE

Geoff Armstrong has suggested that:

> The people employed are the major determinant of corporate competitiveness and success. Management vision is the key to change – vision to create ambitious but achievable goals for the organization and to win the commitment of employees to those goals and to draw from them and their unions their maximum contribution to achieving them.

187

Commitment to the organization's goals means commitment to growth and improving results as measured by the bottom line. Clearly the personnel department has a major part to play in creating an environment and employee relations policies and practices which will engender commitment. This involves the development and implementation of commitment strategies. It also means reviewing the industrial relations scene in order to create more harmonious relationships with trade unions.

COMMITMENT STRATEGY

Basis of commitment strategy

The objectives of the commitment strategy at Nissan were defined as follows:

> Our objective is to establish an atmosphere of mutual trust, co-operation and commitment in which all employees can identify with the aims and objectives of the company and which encourages and recognizes the individual contribution of all.

Richard Walton described the background to commitment strategy in his seminal article in the *Harvard Business Review* as follows:

> Underlying all these (human resource) policies is a management philosophy that acknowledges the legitimate claims of the company's multiple stakeholders – owners, employees, customers and the public. At the centre of this philosophy is a belief that eliciting employee commitment will lead to enhanced performance. This belief is well founded.[1]

He went on to suggest that:

> In this new commitment based approach to the workforce, jobs are designed to be broader than before, to combine planning and implementation, and to include efforts to upgrade operations, not just maintain them. Individual responsibilities are expected to change as conditions change, and teams, not individuals, are often the organizational units accountable for performance. With management hierarchies relatively flat and differences in status minimized, control and lateral co-ordination depend on shared goals and expertise rather than formal position. . . .
> Under the commitment strategy, performance expectations are high and serve not to define minimum standards but to provide 'stretch objectives', emphasize continuous improvement and reflect the requirements of the marketplace.

Aims of commitment strategy

1   *Identification* – Commitment strategy aims to increase the identification of every member of the organization with the mission, goals and core values of that organization.

2   *Mutuality* – The key word is 'mutuality', that is to say, unity of purpose and a shared belief that what is good for the individual is good for the organization and what is good for the organization is good for the individual. Mutuality therefore involves integrating the needs of those who work in the organization with the needs of the organization and an important aim of commitment strategy is to achieve that integration.

3   *Individual creativity and energy* – In developing unity of purpose, commitment strategies aim to unleash the latent creativity and energy of *individuals* throughout the organization. Note the emphasis on individuals. While good teamwork is vital, and a commitment strategy will aim to enhance it, what must not be inferred from the development and application of such a strategy is that the organization wants to create a colony of clones who will slavishly conform to norms and standards imposed on them by the company. As John Harvey-Jones says, it is 'the individual's unique and personal contribution that matters.'[2]

4   *Ownership of change* – Commitment strategy aims to manage change by getting people to 'own' it. This means trying to ensure that those affected by change feel that the project is theirs and not one imposed upon them by outsiders which will conflict with their values or be detrimental in any way.

Components of commitment strategy

To achieve these aims, the components of commitment strategy are:

1   *Statements of purpose and values*. Mission and value statements define the purpose of the organization and its core values. For example, those at Nissan are concerned with teamwork, quality and flexibility, and emphasize that:

   • individual contributions are most effective within a teamworking environment;

   • commitment *at every level* to a zero defect product is the centrepiece of the company's philosophy;

   • continuous improvement is expected from all staff at all times;

   • to ensure the fullest use of facilities and manpower there will be complete flexibility and mobility of employees.

   To be effective, mission and value statements should represent reality – what actually happens, rather than pious intentions. They must be backed up by behaviour which demonstrates that management believes in what it says. And there must be emphasis on the mutual benefits which ensue if the mission is accomplished.

2   *Proclamation of goals.* Everyone should be made aware of the goals of the enterprise, what they are expected to do to achieve them and how they will benefit when they are attained. Employees will be more committed to the organization if they are working towards goals that they accept as legitimate.

3   *Involvement.* People who participate in defining problems and solutions will become committed to the new directions that result from the process of involvement. This can take the form of project teams, working parties, task forces, meetings, quality circles, improvement groups and any other formal or semi-formal ways of bringing people together to develop new ideas, solve problems or manage change. Involvement however, is also an informal process within work groups and the commitment strategy should provide for the encouragement of managers and supervisors to get their people involved, and for training in the approaches they can use.

4   *Communications.* Communication programmes, using all the media available, plus meetings and team briefings can increase understanding and acceptance of management's objectives and values and can get people to identify more closely with the company and its achievements. Communications should cover intentions and proposals (with provision for feedback from employees) as well as achievements and results. The approach should be geared to an understanding by management of what employees want to hear and comment on about matters that affect their interests. This will include such things as the introduction of new technology, the implications of a merger or takeover, and changes in working methods and employment conditions.

5   *Workshops.* These can be part of a systematic programme to get people together to discuss purposefully such things as the company's mission or value statements, its programmes for culture change and its proposals to introduce new technology or working methods. Workshops are different from other forms of involvement or communication in that they will contain a strong element of education and training as well as the opportunity to participate fully in discussions on the whys and wherefores, on how those involved will be affected and what they are expected to do about it.

6   *Training.* Steps should be taken through induction training to ensure that new employees obtain a good impression of the company from the start in terms of its achievements, values and what it offers to them in return for their contributions. Formal continuation training programmes can not only help people to learn new skills but can reinforce favourable attitudes to the company and their work.

7   *Shared objectives.* The key point in Douglas McGregor's theory Y was that 'people will exercise self-direction and self-control in the

achievement of organizational objectives to the degree that they are committed to those objectives.'[3] Commitment will be improved if, throughout the organization, individuals participate in goal setting.

8   *Rewards for performance.* Commitment to agreed objectives is, as McGregor says, 'a function of the rewards associated with their achievement.'[4] Both financial rewards (paying for performance) and non-financial rewards (achievement, recognition, esteem, status, etc) should therefore be related to contribution.

9   *Leadership.* Ralph Waldo Emerson wrote that 'there is no company of men as great as one man' and visionary leadership is a powerful force for creating commitment. Selection, promotion and training programmes must aim to identify, foster and develop leaders who, by inspiration and example, can commit their people to follow them.

10   *Management style.* It is not only leadership which will generate commitment. It is also the total approach that managers adopt in directing, guiding, coaching, motivating and monitoring their staff. The standards of performance for managers should emphasize the importance of this aspect of their role and management training should concentrate on developing the skills required.

11   *Organization and job design.* Commitment will be increased if people are given more responsibility and more freedom to act in an organization which has reduced the number of levels in the hierarchy, minimized or even eliminated status distinctions and operates flexibly.

12   *Environment.* The climate or working atmosphere of the organization can foster commitment if it encourages people's growth in terms of skill and higher levels of achievement, offers them a reasonable degree of stability and security as well as opportunity, eliminates unnecessary barriers such as status distinctions, and is generally friendly, informal and supportive.

Example of commitment strategy

At Borg-Warner Chemicals the task was to manage an acquisition to minimize disruption and maximize commitment to the new owners. The guiding principles set for the acquisition team were:

1   Respect the culture of the company and the country

2   Find synergies at local level

3   Get local management immediately into the new reporting structure

4   Evaluate all personnel procedures

5   Keep your promises, stick to timing and answer questions honestly

6   Communicate! Explain objectives, report on progress and keep the door open for everyone.

The specific objectives of the commitment strategy evolved to support these principles were:

- short term – creating trust through communications
- medium term – creating co-operation and responsibility
- long term – creating the future together as partners.

To help achieve these objectives an employee attitude survey was conducted, a comprehensive communication programme was launched involving free-ranging meetings with all the staff, a new performance related reward system was introduced and the working environment was improved. The maximum amount of freedom was left with the local management team to run the operation and, because trust had been established between them and the new parent company, they were committed to building similar levels of trust throughout the company.

At Motorola a strategy for fostering unity of purpose was based upon the following principles:

- global understanding of fundamental objectives, key beliefs, goals and initiatives;
- acceptance and commitment to fundamental philosophies and values;
- understanding the reasons for changes, actions and decisions;
- breaking down the fences that can grow up in organizations;
- communicating and reinforcing a sense of belonging to the organization.

COMMITMENT AND THE TRADE UNIONS

Trade unions cannot be left out of any bottom-line calculation. The personnel function has the responsibility for providing guidance on strategies and tactics designed to increase harmony, eliminate costly disputes and prevent pay increases getting out of hand.

But the trade union role is changing and as Geoff Armstrong said at an Industrial Society conference in 1988:

> It is no longer starry-eyed to assert that, in a changing world, where products and technologies are increasingly marketed globally against powerful and innovative competitors to powerful and sophisticated customers, UK managers have no option but to compete by continuously finding ways to draw out the skills of employees at all levels. We don't have the choice of going back to adversarial, conflict-based, even class-based ideologies or behaviour. Customers won't let us, and it's right that they shouldn't.

That's not to say that there isn't a role for trade unions, or for collective organizations of people at work, or for collective bargaining on matters affecting their interests – there is: but it has to be based on a joint acceptance of the commercial imperative that an organization that fails to satisfy the needs of customers is dead in the water, however stimulating or enjoyable the negotiators on both sides might have found their industrial relations practices which took them there.

Commitment strategy does not involve ignoring or by-passing the trade unions in their legitimate role of protecting the interests of their members. But as Peter Wickens has said 'employee involvement means involving employees *not* representatives of employees'. Commitment is gained by talking directly to people. And John Guaspari wrote:[5]

Bricks and mortar don't need explanations. Capital equipment never asks why. But people do, and people need answers.

These answers cannot be filtered through trade unions who must accept that their role of advancing as well as protecting the interests of their members will best be achieved if their relationship can be based on partnership, in the interests of all concerned, rather than on contention.

References

1   WALTON, Richard. 'From control to commitment in the workplace'. *Harvard Business Review*, March–April 1985. pp 77–84
2   HARVEY-JONES, John. *Making it happen.* Glasgow, Collins, 1988
3   McGREGOR, Douglas. *The human side of enterprise.* New York, McGraw-Hill, 1960
4   *Ibid.*
5   GUASPARI, John. 'The role of human resources in selling quality involvement to employees'. *Management Review.* American Management Association, 1987

15 Personnel and the Bottom Line: Conclusions

The theme of this book has been that personnel management in the 1990s will be essentially an entrepreneurial function which is built into the fabric of market-orientated and profit-conscious businesses. The objectives and activities of the personnel function need to be developed from and integrated with the needs of the business as expressed by its mission statement, its strategic plans and its programmes for achieving corporate goals.

In any organization, people are the ultimate source of value. Personnel management activities have a major impact on individual performance and therefore must also impact on productivity and organizational performance as measured by the bottom line. They do this by taking a strategic view of human resource management, by helping to shape the culture and values of the organization, by facilitating change and by ensuring that they promote commitment and the successful pursuit of quality and excellence.

Personnel managers are enablers with a sense of purpose. That purpose is to further the achievement of business goals by the effective procurement, development and motivation of the resource which is instrumental in attaining these goals – the people employed in the organization.

Personnel managers contribute to the formulation of corporate strategies as business partners. They know that their companies exist to achieve demanding objectives expressed in bottom-line terms. They are change agents, involved in helping the organization to innovate, grow and build competitive advantage. They appreciate that the organization has to obtain added value from its human resources. They aim to be 'profit effective' by evaluating everything they do in terms of its impact, direct or indirect, on the bottom line. Their bias is towards actions which produce measurable improvements in performance. Although they will be concerned to provide cost-effective personnel services, and may have to play a part in cost-reduction exercises which result in down-sizing, they will be much more orientated to taking a positive approach to the improvement of productivity (achieving better ratios between outputs and inputs) than to adopting a negative cost-reduction attitude.

The point has been made that a business, bottom-line orientation should not preclude personnel managers continuing to pay close attention to the

194

social responsibilities of the organization. These are to provide working life of the highest possible quality, to create a healthy, safe and pleasant working environment, to provide as much security and continuity of employment as possible, to give people opportunities to grow with the organization and to treat them fairly and with consideration. Personnel managers should be entrepreneurs, but entrepreneurs with a human face.

IMPACT ON THE BOTTOM LINE

In order to have an impact on the bottom line, the personnel function must:

1 Foster a performance-orientated environment which instills a sense of purpose in all members of the organization and stimulates creativity, enterprise and endeavour.

2 Create a 'culture of pride and success' and a value-driven organization which encourages high levels of commitment, performance, competence, flexibility, innovation, quality and customer service.

3 Develop unified vision in an organization which will increasingly be staffed by specialists. This is achieved by developing integrative strategies which support co-operation and teamwork, clarify and stress the interdependence of activities, create interdisciplinary teams with shared objectives and ensure that everyone knows how his or her efforts will contribute to the achievement of corporate objectives.

4 Understand that continuous renewal is a requirement forced on organizations by commercial pressures, technological development and the emergence of the global firm.

5 Appreciate that in these circumstances cultural change and the recruitment and development of entrepreneurial and innovative people are processes which have to be planned and implemented if the firm is to build and maintain competitive advantage.

6 Articulate the agenda for change and use the personnel function as a lever for its achievement.

7 Be fully aware of the steps that need to be taken by the organization to grow profitably, building on present capacities and strengths.

8 Set the direction of human resource strategy deliberately and consciously as an integral and key part of the business strategy.

9 Develop organization structures which encourage flexibility, teamwork, effective inter-action and rapid responses to new situations.

10 Help to develop flatter and leaner organizations which operate close to their markets and encourage entrepreneurial activity.

11 Recognize that operations in the new flexible, responsive and market-orientated firms will often best be carried out by task forces.

This means understanding that these task forces will cut across traditional organizational boundaries and, therefore, will have to be managed with great care, without unduly interfering with their freedom. Such management will involve the highest skills of integrative leadership, the setting of explicit output targets and the clarification of any constraints that may have to be accepted by the task forces in carrying out their tasks.

12   Understand that it is people who create added value in organizations and invest in them accordingly.

13   Identify the competences required to achieve the goals set out in the strategic plan and ensure that resourcing programmes provide the organization with people who can operate effectively at the leading edge.

14   Know that high-level performers are in short supply and that such shortages will be exacerbated by impending demographic problems. Anticipate these problems by restructuring jobs, encouraging flexibility and multi-skilling and introducing new technology so that the demand for scarce skills will diminish. Plan new training or retraining programmes to supply these skills or boost their availability. Recognize the growing importance of part-timers, contract workers and homeworkers while appreciating that the organization and planning of their work will present special problems which can only be solved by more flexible methods of operation.

15   Understand that high-level performers will be attracted to and will stay with the organization if they know that they will be given plenty of opportunity to grow with it.

16   Make sure that in the flatter organizations those who cannot see a promotion ladder know that there will still be plenty of opportunities for them to develop their careers as professionals or specialists in a growth environment.

17   Take steps to develop a flexible approach to work by providing opportunities for growth and enlargement of responsibilities.

18   Invest heavily in performance-related training as a means of supplying the required skills and achieving better bottom-line results.

19   Introduce objective-setting systems which establish stretching targets and act as levers for the attainment of higher standards of performance.

20   Develop performance-management systems which appraise and reward people not only on the basis of short-term individual achievements but also on their contributions to achieving longer-term goals, and on their ability to work effectively as part of a team.

21   Recognize that in an enterprise culture pay levels will be market-driven and that competitive resourcing policies may require the payment of

market rates at some expense to the principle of internal equity. At the same time, however, deviations from this principle should be controlled so that they occur only when no other alternative is possible.

22   Plan and maintain continuous drives to make the achievement of total quality and high levels of customer service ways of life.

23   Where appropriate, take steps to introduce people to the global aspects of the organization by giving them responsibilities for some aspect of international business or by periodic transfers or attachments abroad.

24   Scrutinize all aspects of personnel activities to check that they are adding value, are cost-effective and are supporting the achievement of the bottom-line targets of the enterprise.

25   Take a positive approach to the improvement of productivity through the effective utilization of human resources.

Index

Abbey National 117, 146, 173–4
Added value xi, 15, 27, 84–5
Alliance and Leicester Building
  Society 173
Ambiguity 10, 50–1
Armstrong, Geoff 23, 34, 97, 125–8,
  187, 192–3
Armstrong, Michael 16
Artificial intelligence 5
Athos, Anthony 4, 24

Beattie, Don 37, 58–9, 114–5, 123,
  138, 159–60, 174
Beckhard, Richard 134
Birley, Sue 156, 158
Book Club Associates 27–8, 33–4,
  36, 41, 81, 95, 100–1, 133, 138,
  144–5
Bottom line, the xi, 1, 9, 15, 16, 17,
  18, 26, 27, 30, 39, 48, 55, 70, 84,
  93, 108, 165
  (and) commitment 187–8
  factors affecting 81–83
  (and) human resource
    development 145–55
  (and) human resource planning
    138–40
  impact of personnel function on
    195–7
  planning and budgeting for 85–9
  (and) reward management 170–1
Borg-Warner Chemicals 191–2
Boston Consulting Group 6, 142
Bowen, Hank 59, 152–3
British Airways 111, 172
Budgeting 87, 88

Burns, Tom 131
Business plan 36, 92, 141
  (see also corporate strategy)

Cadbury Schweppes 19, 22, 34–5,
  41, 64, 79–80, 99, 118–20, 150–1,
  163–4, 169–70
Canavan, Patrick 9
Career planning 152–4
Chandler, A 132, 142
Change, see culture change
Chapman, Rhiannon 18, 34, 40, 50,
  51, 59–61, 124–5
Climate, see organization climate
Collectivism 3
Commitment 10, 17, 20, 41, 86, 93
  (and the) bottom line 187–8
  definition of 187
  strategy for 189–192
  (and the) trade unions 192–3
Communications 190
Competences 12, 142–5, 163–4
Competitive advantage xi, 43, 53, 85
Competitive edge 4, 15, 180
Coopers & Lybrand 5, 99
Core values, see values
Corporate culture 26, 28, 41, 67, 79,
  93
  culture change 109–16
  definition of 103
  (as a) lever for change 108–9
  relevance of 108
  (and) resourcing 137–8
Corporate plan 95–97
Corporate strategy 55, 64
Cost-effectiveness 19

Cowan, Nick   16, 31, 35, 100, 183, 186
Crosby, John   22, 45, 61–2
Culture, see corporate culture
Culture change
  change strategies   111
  (and) performance management 158
  (the) process of change   109
  programmes for change   109–11
  requirements for success   112–16
Cummins Engine   27
Curnow, Barry   17–18, 47–8, 53–4, 62, 83–4, 136, 137–8, 168
Customer care programmes   184–5
Customers   xi, 7, 27, 85

Davis, Tom   77
Deal, T F   116
Demographic change   2, 140–1
Digital   113
Drucker, Peter   9, 73, 93, 160

Edwardes, Sir Michael   53
Employee involvement, see involvement
Employee relations   86, 93
Enterprise culture   1, 3, 10, 16, 24
Entrepreneurial approach to personnel management   27–8, 55, 58–9, 75–8
Entrepreneurs   15, 85
Environmental change   1–2
Excellence   7, 24, 180
Executive reward strategy   174
Expectancy theory   165–166, 167

Fell, Alan   22–3, 52–3, 62–3, 75–6, 78, 96, 140
Ford Motor Company   84, 98, 120–1
Fowler, Alan   171–3

Geneen, Harold   9
General Electric   142, 151–2
General Foods   27
Gilder, George   2, 15
Goal theory   166
Guaspari, John   193
Guest, David   22

Halfords, 64–6
Handy, Charles   11–12
Harvey-Jones, Sir John   10, 189
Hay job evaluation scheme   144–5

Hewlett Packard   27, 77, 113, 180
High performance work design   11
Hobbs, Peter   32, 38, 63, 74, 76, 97, 115–6, 149
Hougham, John   35–6, 84, 98, 120–1, 130–1
Human resource development   21, 23
Human resource management   xi, 20, 22, 26–27
Human resource planning   23, 67, 98, 138–42
Human resource strategy
  aims of   91–2
  areas of   93
  as part of business plan   92
  check list   90–93
  content of   97–101
  (and the) corporate plan   95–7
  formation of   94–5
  need for   52
  role of   93–4

Iacocca, Lee   8
IBM   27, 74, 113, 121, 172
ICL   7, 115, 121–4, 159–60, 174
Individualism   3, 10
Industrial relations   21
Information technology   9, 12, 45
International Stock Exchange   43–4, 59–61, 124–5
Intrapreneurs   28, 85
Involvement   42, 190

Japanese   4
Joseph, Sir Keith   2
Just in time (JIT)   5–6

Kanter, Rosabeth Moss   11, 17, 26, 112, 132, 168, 171
Kennedy, A   116
Kirkman, Mike   125–8

Lawler, E E   165
Legal and General   46
Legge, Karen   186
Levitt, Theodore   4
LIFO   107
Locke, F A   166

Mackay, L   39
Management by objectives   160–1
Management development   86, 149–55

Management style 106–7
Manpower planning 37
    see also human resource planning
Market economy 3
Marketing 4, 6–7
MB (Metal Box) Group 125–8
McGregor, Douglas 190–1
Miles, R F 158
Miller, Paul 26
Mintzberg, Henry 95
Mission 30
Motivating strategy 166–7
Motorola 9–10, 192
MSL Group 62
Murphy, Terry 16, 36, 46–7, 76, 97,
    117, 146, 150, 176
Mutuality 17, 20–21, 189

National Health Service 161–2
National Westminster Bank 172
New technology 5, 11, 17
Niche marketing 4
Nissan 4, 67–8, 182, 187
Norms, cultural 103, 104

Organization behaviour 107
Organization climate 105–6
Organization development 24,
    134–5
Organization planning
    achieving the aims 130
    aims 130
    organization development 134–5
    problems and opportunities 131–3
Organization structure 16–17, 20,
    93, 107
Ouchi, William 24

Pascale, Richard 4, 24
Paying for performance 10–11, 86
    issues 175–6
    performance related pay 177–9
    relationship with appraisal 177
    trends in 171–2
Peach, Sir Leonard 31–2, 40, 112,
    121, 139, 141, 161, 176–7
Performance 16, 32–3
Performance appraisal
    achievement rating 162
    aims of 161–2
    analysis of strengths and
        weaknesses 163
    competency approach 163–4
    performance improvement 161

    requirements for success 164–5
Performance management 34, 86,
    93
    definition of 156
    motivating strategy 166–7
    need for 156–7
    performance appraisal 161–6
    performance improvement 15
    process of 157–8
    reward management 168–79
Performance related pay 177–9
Performance related training 86,
    145–8
Personnel directors
    contribution of 59–60
    (as) entrepreneurs 55, 70
    evaluation of 67
    influence of 65–6
    job description 56–7
    objectives of 60–1
    priorities of 62–3
    role of 21, 48, 55–7, 58, 63, 68–9
    skills of 68
    (and) strategy 68
Personnel function
    entrepreneurial nature of 30
    growth in 2
    impact on bottom line 79–89,
        195–7
    objectives of 40–44
    organization of 45–8
    (and) quality 185–6
    role of 17–18, 32, 34, 35–6, 38,
        44–8
    staffing of 45–48
Personnel managers
    (and) ambiguity 50–5
    bottom line contribution 30, 70
    (and) cultural change 113–114
    (as) entrepreneurs 15–16, 75–8
    (as) facilitators 71
    (as) interventionists 71–2
    (as) performance managers xi
    qualities of 53–4, 78
    role of 21, 35, 39, 70, 73–4
Personnel planning 86, 88
Personnel strategy
    see human resource strategy
Peters, Tom 1, 7, 15, 21, 24
Philips 183
Planning, see business planning,
    human resource planning and
    personnel planning
Popper, Sir Karl 73, 80

Porter, L W   165
Processes   37–8, 134–5
Proctor and Gamble   27
Productivity   87–9
Profit   xi, 81, 86, 87, 93–4

Quality   17, 180–3

Reay, Peter   22, 41–2, 45–6, 64,
    79–80, 99, 112, 118–20, 133
Resourcing
  competitive resourcing   136
  corporate culture development
    137–8
  (and) performance management
    158–9
  strategies for   93, 136–7
Reward management
  (and the) bottom line   170–1
  concept of   168–9
  (and) culture change   111
  executive reward strategy   174
  paying for performance   17, 109
  strategy for   169–70
Richards, Lynn   64–6, 80, 146
Roberts, Jeff   35, 66–7, 128–9
Rumbelows   66–7, 128–9

Sapsed, Gordon   74, 121
Say, J B   15
Schein, Ed   116
Shell U K Oil   43
Skae, John   46
Smiles, Samuel   2
Smith, Adam   2
Smith, W H plc   59, 144, 146–7,
    152–4
Snow, C C   158
Social change   2–3
Social engineering   73, 80, 84
Social responsibility   xi, 80, 194–5

Stalker, G M   131
Stanton, Mike   40, 51, 71, 99,
    112–14, 138–9
Strategy, see corporate strategy,
    personnel strategy and human
    resource strategy
Systems   107–8
Systems approach   37

Teamwork   10
Texas Instruments   27, 142
Thorn EMI   99–100
Time-based competition   6
Toffler, Alvin   11
Torrington, D   39
Trade unions   2, 84, 192–3
Training   86, 190
    see also performance related
    training
TSB   100
Tyson, Shaun   22–3, 53, 63

Unilever   67, 154

Values   38–9, 40, 41, 79
  definition of core values   103–5
Vineall, Tony   21, 67, 71–3, 78, 114,
    136, 154, 156–7

Walton, R   10, 17, 188
Warwick University   20, 52
Waterman, Robert   7, 15, 24
Wellcome Foundation   63
Wickens, Peter   4, 19, 44–5, 67–8,
    81, 94, 133, 180, 193
Work, nature of   11–12
Workshops 111, 190

Young, Don   32–3, 37, 68, 74,
    99–100